This ingenious exercise in lite
provides the definitive solution to
have tantalized fans of Edgar Allar
The controversy over his apparer
character, the violent critical att.

barred long after his death, the scandal surround-
Nabokov-Wilson confronta... ... a ... . Fllet—to all these
welterweights. Above all, he presents .... -lation-
faceted portrait of the mercurial Fanny ·
though adulated by the general pub'· · ...
known and . ' ' -1 b-· ...-rc h ·
the s· ' ·

Also by
John Evangelist Walsh

The Shroud:
The Story of the Holy Shroud of Turin

Strange Harp, Strange Symphony:
The Life of Francis Thompson

The Letters of Francis Thompson

Poe the Detective:
The Curious Circumstances Behind
The Mystery of Marie Roget

The Hidden Life of Emily Dickinson

One Day at Kitty Hawk:
The Untold Story of the Wright Brothers

Night on Fire:
The First Complete Account of
John Paul Jones' Greatest Battle

Plumes in the Dust

The Love Affair of
Edgar Allan Poe
and
Fanny Osgood

Plumes in the Dust

The Love Affair of
Edgar Allan Poe
and
Fanny Osgood

by
John Evangelist Walsh

Nelson-Hall nh Chicago

Library of Congress Cataloging in Publication Data

Walsh, John Evangelist, 1927–
  Plumes in the dust.

  Bibliography: p.
  Includes index.
   1. Poe, Edgar Allan, 1809–1849—Relationship
with women—Fanny Osgood. 2. Osgood, Frances
Sargent Locke, 1811–1850—Relationship with men—
Edgar Allan Poe. 3. Authors, American—19th
century—Biography. I. Title.
PS2632.W3 818′.309   79–27534
ISBN 0–88229–683–3

Manufactured in the United States of America

10 9 8 7 6 5 4 3 2 1

For
Mandy

I must go down into the depths and
shy recesses of time, over which dusky
draperies are hanging and voluminous
curtains have long since fallen.

> De Quincey, *Paper on*
> *Sir William Hamilton*

Nothing definite *can* be known
And vague rumors will soon
be forgotten.

> Mrs. Ellet to
> Mrs. Osgood,
> July 8, 1846

Contents

But Psyche, uplifting her finger,
  Said—"Sadly this star I mistrust—
  Her pallor I strangely mistrust—
Ah, hasten!—ah, let us not linger!
  Ah, fly!—let us fly!—for we must.
In terror she spoke; letting sink her
  Wings till they trailed in the dust—
In agony sobbed; letting sink her
  Plumes till they trailed in the dust—
  Till they sorrowfully trailed in the dust.

                    From "Ulalume"

Prologue

It still stands there, the Poe house at 85 Amity Street in New York City, sagging a little, its tired bricks much worn, but looking nearly as it did when Poe, his wife and his mother-in-law went daily up and down its front steps to their apartment on the second floor. Of course the passage of a century-and-a-third has brought many changes to the street. It is now prosaically called West Third, the rough cobblestones of former days are covered by asphalt, and some taller, more massive buildings surge above the line of the older, narrower roofs. And no one lives at No. 85 now. The Poe apartment, like the others, is used for storage. Occupying the ground floor is a saloon. It is called the Gold Bug.

Very fitting is the preservation of No. 85 when so much else connected with Poe in Manhattan has been swept away. While living here he enjoyed his first taste of real celebrity, after publication of "The Raven," as well as some of his all too rare moments of settled home life. Here also there occurred a number of the more crucial incidents of his career, chief among which is the notorious affair of Mrs. Ellet's

letters. It was this unfortunate interlude, still known only
in dim outline, that was to bring an abrupt change to his
life, driving him in vague disgrace from Amity Street and
out of the city. When, after some six months residence, Poe
moved away from No. 85 with his sick wife and mother-in-
law, his rise to fame had passed its meridian, and his reputation had been permanently tarnished. Thereafter he was
to be in many ways a lonelier and less happy man. Within
a year his wife would die. Within four years he would meet
his own death, raving on a hospital bed.

The Ellet affair, as has long been known but too often
forgotten, arose in the first place out of Poe's association with
a married woman, Mrs. Frances Sargent Osgood, a popular
poet of the time whose name was briefly linked with his in
the gossip of literary circles. Ever since, the fleeting presence
of Fanny Osgood has continued to haunt Poe biography—
though the true nature of her role in the Ellet affair, and in
Poe's life generally, remained tantalizingly out of reach. It
was only in fairly recent days, with the surfacing of one further fact, that the hidden pattern began to emerge. That
fact concerns a shadowy child, born to Fanny in 1846, and
about whose paternity there seems to have been doubt from
the start. With the forgotten child as clue, much that had
been murky becomes clear, for circumstances point irresist-
ibly to Poe being the father. And that long suppressed fact,
spreading its implications forward and back, goes far toward
clarifying some other curious incidents involving Poe and
Fanny.

There was, for instance, the charge of forgery leveled
against Poe, whispered into Fanny's delicate ear, by a man
Poe had never met—a charge which was to lead, if indirectly,
to the only lawsuit of his career. There was the outrageous
hoax he perpetrated at the Boston Lyceum, presenting as a
new and original poem one of his earliest works, an incident
through which there again floats Fanny's aethereal presence.
In particular, there was the hectic and hurried visit he paid

to Fanny in Albany soon after the death of his wife, during which he begged her hand in marriage, while seemingly ignoring the fact that she already had a husband.

But the most important development of all, perhaps, is the sudden and starkly revealing light thrown upon all that strange violence, that actual hatred, with which Poe's character was posthumously assailed. It was no accident, it now can be seen, that those who most bitterly denounced him after his death arose from among the vulnerable Fanny's warmest admirers. The two men who were to vent their rage most damningly against his memory—Rufus Griswold and Richard Henry Stoddard—had both enjoyed particularly intimate friendships with her. Griswold was a frequent visitor at the Osgood home; he repeatedly extolled Fanny's writings as among the finest in the country, and at the end he comforted her death bed. The career of the young and fiercely ambitious Stoddard received early and frequent encouragement from her. It is surprising, to say the least, that the long-time effort to uncover the true sources of the slashing bitterness that these two, especially, unleashed against the dead Poe has overlooked the link with Fanny Osgood.

Beyond all that, still another fact, hitherto unsuspected, becomes compellingly clear. That unique poem "Ulalume," which has for so long called forth the admiration of the critics, or their sneers, while considerably exercising their ingenuity, almost certainly received its first inspiration not from the grieved memory of some immortal love, or from Poe's own heated imagination, but from the sad death at the age of sixteen months of Fanny's baby.

In my effort to piece together the truth of all these things I have clung with some fervor to the primary documents in the case. I have chosen, however, to present the results of my study for the most part in the form of a straight narrative, relating the facts as they have come together in my own understanding, and not always pausing to explain or qualify. In such fashion, I feel, largely because of the tangled skein to be unwound, my argument is more effectively, and I hope more attractively, presented. But the proof of my fidelity to sources, even in speculation, along with explanations of my reasoning, will be found fully arrayed in the extensive notes. There, my weaving of the facts, my assumptions, assertions and conclusions may be fully tested.

If the pattern of events as here reconstructed is valid, then the last major blank in that often somber though curiously triumphant career has been filled up. Yet that, in the usual way of Poe matters, is only to say that still another door has been opened. For in the long hidden events of this period, I am convinced, lay the seed of much that was unfortunate in Poe's behavior afterward. Had there been no Fanny Osgood to break up the congealed fountains of his resigned heart, and no Mrs. Ellet to agitate poor, stricken Virginia, then there might have been no Helen Whitman, perhaps no Elmira Shelton. Nor, probably, would Poe have died how and when he did. But that is another story.

1.
Region of Sighs

The bitter night winds of February, blowing in off the chill waters of New York harbor, shrilled north along lower Broadway, blasting icicles and swirls of snow from the ledges of buildings. While the intense cold had driven most people indoors, at the southeast corner of Broadway and Leonard Street a steady straggle of bundled up men and women hurried through the ornate stone doorway of the New York Society Library.

Inside, they filed into a small auditorium where the soft glow of whale-oil lamps lit a narrow stage. By eight o'clock some three hundred seats had been filled, about half the capacity of the room. It was an elite audience, made up mostly of editors and writers from the city's thirty or so daily and weekly newspapers and magazines, as well as a large contingent of New York authors. They had gathered to hear Edgar Allan Poe deliver some frank opinions on the poets and poetry of America, but it was not solely Poe's reputation as a critic that had drawn these men and women from their firesides on that blustery night. Many had come simply

to ogle the town's newest celebrity. A month before, in the
New York Mirror, Poe had published his latest poem, "The
Raven," and, as one observer said, sophisticated New York
had gone "raven-mad."

The man they now saw, his head and shoulders showing
above the lectern, at the age of thirty-six was the embodi-
ment of the Romantic poet. An imposing brow rose above
shadowed eyes, the sensitive face tapering to a delicately
squared chin. The hair, dark brown and slightly waving,
parted on the left side, curled in back to the top of his
collar. In his low voice there sounded an elusive musical
quality which with a crisp delivery somehow imparted a
charming impression of mingled warmth and rigor. After a
few general remarks on the lamentable state of American
poetry, and the even more deplorable state of American
criticism, Poe began singling out certain leading poets for
discussion. Briefly he sketched estimates of Bryant, Longfellow, and half a dozen others. None drew unqualified
praise. A few, such as Dana and Sprague, he cast aside with
a disdainful sentence or two.

The female poets were discussed as a group, beginning
with Lydia Sigourney, who was given a high accolade, and
Amelia Welby, also accorded superior rank. Then he annoyed
his listeners by deprecating the verses of the popular Davidson sisters, both of whom had died in their teens a few years
before and who were then enjoying posthumous fame on
both sides of the ocean. The work of the sisters was negligible, Poe explained, their fame only the passing result of
a sentimental reaction to their premature deaths.

The final woman he had chosen to mention was the pro-
lific Frances Sargent Osgood, and for her his praise was un-
stinted. In originality, in piquant diction, even in technical
skills, he found her the equal of all other women poets and
superior to most. She possessed a happy refinement, he said,
an exquisite instinct of the pure, the delicate. Perhaps in the
loftier merits she was not yet the equal of, say, Mrs. Welby

or Mrs. Brooks. But in that indescribable something called *grace,* she was without a peer. At no distant time, he predicted, Mrs. Osgood would stand alone, both in popularity and in the secure fame of immortal works. This enthusiastic praise of the woman who was familiarly known to many in the hall as Fanny was greeted by loud applause.

In the audience, a fascinated listener, sat William Gillespie, twenty-six-year-old teacher of mathematics, sometime poet and writer of travel books. As Poe came to a close, Gillespie hurried out, boarded a Broadway omnibus going downtown and a few minutes later stepped off in front of the Astor House, opposite City Hall. Inside, in the elegant lounge, he walked up to a woman who was seated by herself in a corner. Two hours earlier he had left her there, awaiting the friend who would escort her to the lecture. Missing her from the room, Gillespie had hastened back to report the magnificent praise she had received from the austere critic. Mr. Poe had predicted great things for her: she would someday stand first among the female writers of the country! Trying to recall the phrases Poe had used, Gillespie told how the audience had heartily seconded the prediction.

Fanny Osgood, her large gray eyes sparkling, listened closely, on her face a mingling of joy and doubt—no critic before had hailed the promise of her work in so serious a fashion. But while she expressed polite demurrers to Gillespie, her heart was singing. None even of her many intimate friends had guessed at the real ambition that smoldered behind those calm, bright, ever-playful eyes.

After the lecture, Poe caught an omnibus going uptown. Rumbling north on Broadway behind a shivering team of horses, his mind still churning with the evening's effort, he must have known some measure of contentment. On this night of February 28, 1845, he was one of the best-known critics in America, even if one of the most controversial. Ideas for stories and articles were swarming in his imagination. Every day he spent productive hours in his office at the

Broadway Journal, every night he worked steadily at his own writing. And if he never composed another stanza, it had been said, "The Raven" would assure him undying renown. But of course he would write more, even better and more important things than "The Raven," he had no doubt of that. The true reach of his mind, always felt in potential, was only now beginning to reveal itself.

At the corner of Broadway and Amity Street, a block below Washington Square, he alighted from the omnibus and walked east. At No. 15, a large, old-fashioned building whose faded grandeur was reflected in the massive stoop and huge windows, he entered the darkened doorway and mounted the stairs to an apartment on the second floor, rear.*

The next afternoon there arrived at Amity Street a short note signed by William Gillespie. At this time the two had not met, but Poe would have recognized the name as the author of a travel book he had reviewed at length in the *Broadway Journal* a couple of weeks before.

My Dear Sir,

I was one of your delighted hearers last night, but I have to complain that you tempted me to load my memory with so many points of thought and expression, that I carried off very imperfectly one passage which I particularly desired to remember—your characterization of Mrs. Osgood. I had left her in the Astor House with her hat on awaiting the friend with whom she was coming to the lecture; but she was disappointed, and lost the pleasure of hearing you, which she had so eagerly anticipated, though not knowing that she would be noticed. I fear that she was not sufficiently *en rapport* with me to share my thrill of pleasure at the passage, and the applause which followed it; and therefore I ask of you the favor of giving me an opportunity to copy it from your manuscript, as I should be unwilling to give you that trouble.

---

*The Poes lived on Amity Street twice during 1845: first, during the spring, at No. 15, and in the fall at No. 85. In between, they resided for a short time at 195 East Broadway.

Poe promptly replied with an invitation to Gillespie to
drop in at the *Journal* office. He might also have shrewdly
guessed that it was not so much Gillespie, but Fanny herself
who longed to read the exact terms of the lavish praise he
had bestowed on her in the hearing of all the literary lights
of New York City.

At thirty-four Fanny Osgood had been married for ten
years and was the mother of two small daughters, Ellen, nine,
and May, six. Her husband was Samuel Stilman Osgood,
thirty-seven, a leading portrait painter. The two were pres-
ently estranged.

They had met and fallen in love in 1834, when Sam was
commissioned by her family to do a portrait of the youthful
Fanny. While she posed, he talked, making her head swim
with romantic tales about his early days as an itinerant
painter, his adventures in Europe and South America, his
thrilling escape from a fearsome shipwreck. Someday, he told
her, he would throw aside his lucrative but soul-dimming
sketching of the idle rich. He would devote his art to grander
scenes and subjects.

The attraction Sam felt was not solely physical, for Fanny
was by no means beautiful in the conventional way. Her nose
was too long, her mouth a touch too narrow, her chin a
trifle pointed and prominent. But the hair was thick and
black and glossy, the elongated oval of the face was flawless
and there were compelling depths in the large, lucent eyes.
Though she was scarcely taller than a child, perhaps an inch
or two over five feet, there was a peculiar natural grace to
the movements of her fragile figure, making her seem just a
bit aethereal. The total effect was compelling. Many people
after a first meeting remembered her as an authentic beauty,
only to be surprised on seeing her again to find they had
been mistaken.

The two married and went to live in London, where Fanny
wrote and published poetry while Sam continued to apply
his brush to portraiture, unable to retreat from money-

making. By the time they returned to settle in New York, in 1840, Sam was spending more and more time in the company of his clients, their wives and daughters, as well as frequenting a more Bohemian set. After about three years, they began living apart, Fanny and her daughters mostly at the Astor House, from where they made frequent trips to her relatives in Providence, and Sam at his studio on Sixteenth Street.

While the separation was distressing for Fanny, her loneliness was relieved by the crowd of friends and admirers that soon flocked around her. Many were writers, journalists, poets and would-be poets, all accustomed to celebrating each other in verse. Before long they were composing tributes to Fanny's unworldliness, her grace, her finely-strung nature, her purity, her generous heart, and particularly, as one verse proclaimed, her "scorn of all things mean." While the tributes were sincere, by a not uncommon irony, it appears that the very qualities thus hymned were much the same ones that had irritated, wearied and driven away her husband.

In or out of literature there can have been few more contradictory personalities than that of Fanny Osgood. A sympathetic listener and wise counsellor to her friends, she was blessed with a rare and sensitive intellect—"the finest intelligence," said one admirer, "that any woman of the time had brought to the ministry of the beautiful." Yet in her daily attitude, and frequently in her behavior, there was a childlike impulsiveness, a discordant fey quality that often descended to something startlingly infantile. Seemingly in a moment, Fanny would pass from a smiling, mature woman to a capricious child, producing an effect little short of grotesque. One friend recalled bringing her some unfortunate news from Providence, which he thought would elicit a concerned response. Fire had destroyed the barn of a close neighbor, he told Fanny. She stared briefly, then clasped her hands at her back, spun coyly around on her heel and chanted, "Don't care! Don't care!" Such sudden transformations, while sometimes drawing surprised laughter from the beholder, remained disconcerting. Once at a party a woman friend took Fanny aside and gently chided her for being rather too free in her conversation with some young gentlemen. She would be misunderstood, warned the friend. Sinking to her knees beside the friend's chair, Fanny's face took on a little-girl pout, and she placed a shy kiss on the woman's shoulder. "Yes, always by the dull and envious," she sighed. "Shelter me under your wings, Eva, I never can go the dignified."

This incongruous blend of high intellect and childish ways is remarked on by all who knew her. While its total effect is impossible now to recover, either in spite of it or because of it, she was able to inspire intense friendships among both women and men. Apparently the women responded to what they saw as sweetness, innocence and purity of heart, the men to her impulsive trust, her ardent disregard of worldly tact —better described as sauciness—and a sensitivity that at times actually quivered. To nearly everyone in her circle she seemed "a weird, tender child whom one wanted to shelter . . . so fragile, so dependent that maternity looked distorted upon her."

As a writer of short fiction, even in most of her poetry, Fanny was relentlessly autobiographical, frequently including at least a portion of herself in the picture, and more often she was at center stage. It was in one of her short stories, published just now, that she provided a miniature of herself and her husband that was unerringly recognized by all who knew her:

> He regarded his wife with fondness and admiration, but she was far too pure, too aerial, too finely organized for his rougher and warmer temperament. . . . He did not know what to make of the exquisite fragility, the timid sensitiveness of the creature confided to his keeping. . . . If his manly voice took unconsciously a colder or more careless tone, those great gray eyes would be raised pleadingly, implor-

ingly to his. . . . If he breathed a word of praise, a quick
vivid blush would burn and fade in her pure cheek, so suddenly that it startled him. If he frowned, the graceful lip
would quiver and the soft eyes close.

Since Fanny played the child even with her husband, it
is not surprising that with her two spritelike daughters she
did very much the same. At times she would shower them
with attention, caressing them, romping and playing games
with them, telling them made-up stories, showing them off,
as a friend recalled, as if they were "delightful puppets."
Then someone or something would catch her attention, for
hours or days, and the little girls would be left to the care
of a friend or a nurse. One of her most intimate acquaintances was to say of her that, while Fanny did love her children and didn't mean to neglect them, she was simply lacking in ordinary maternal instincts. "I never could bear to
think of Fanny as a mother," confessed the friend.

Through everything she wrote constantly, verse and short
stories, urged on by the ready acceptance given her work in
a dozen magazines. In metrical composition she was strik-
ingly facile, with words, rhymes and images flowing easily
from her pen. If an idea struck her, she would, and frequently did, write even when surrounded by company, scribbling in a corner on slips of paper or an old envelope. Among
her friends there was a suspicion that she needed the hum-
ming of conversation around her in order to compose, that
she was somehow unnerved by solitude.

Her poetry was light, sentimental, songlike. Only occasionally did there chime out some finer note, to be quickly sub-
merged again in froth. To some extent she was already
aware that her easy facility in the lighter forms of verse, that
talent which so impressed her friends, was really the enemy
of a worthier achievement, repeatedly luring her into small
victories. Profoundly she felt what she called "immortal
yearnings," lovingly she nurtured the hope that still somehow she might win undying laurels. In a brief poem written

about now she ringingly exhorts herself to "thy loftiest song," and insists:

> I know my soul is strong and high
>   If once I give it sway;
> I feel a glorious power within,
>   Tho' light I seem, and gay.

Perhaps, she dimly wondered, what she required was some powerful outside force, some sudden elemental influence from afar, that would strike as lightning into her cloudy soul, suffusing it with sharp, unnative brilliance—a visitation, she thought, that might come to her from some other, more fertile mind. It was in this mood of yearning that she had received the news of Poe's exciting predictions for her future, and her reaction was inevitable. She must meet, she must talk with this inspiring critic. Her friend Nathaniel Willis, of the *New York Mirror*, was also a friend and former employer of Poe. Within a week after the lecture an appointment was set, cleverly arranged by Willis as an invitation from Poe for Fanny to read and comment on "The Raven."

The meeting took place in the lounge of the Astor House. Fanny, approaching the two waiting men, gazed at Poe and decided that he was not only handsome but that his face had a remarkable spiritual quality, the shadowed eyes aflash with ardent thought. This was something for which she had not been prepared by the engraved portrait of him that had lately appeared in *Graham's* magazine—the article that accompanied the portrait had seemed to hint at grimness.

Suddenly unsure of herself, Fanny responded to Willis's introduction with a blush and a stammered greeting. Poe's unexpectedly grave, almost cold manner only deepened her confusion, but when he spoke, his tone warm and earnest, she began to feel at ease.

The three sat and talked for a while, then Willis left. For another hour or so, Fanny and Poe discussed poets and poetry, his as well as hers, especially "The Raven," which

Fanny confessed she had found "strange and thrilling, sounding of unearthly music." Quite soon, Fanny began to feel the power of Poe's personality, the subtle charm felt by so many of the women of his acquaintance. "He spoke in a low voice," a friend recalled, "without any sympathetic vibration, yet it was one you listened to hear again. . . . He liked to fall into a sort of eloquent monologue, half dream, half poetry. . . . Men were intolerant of all this but women fell under its fascination and listened in silence."

When they parted after that first meeting, Fanny was elated. It seemed that she had already touched unsuspected depths of heart and mind, visited regions of poetry undreamt before. Almost immediately she hastened to put the experience into a short story, and in the thoughts of her fictional heroine she betrayed the sweet agitation stirring in her own breast. "I do not think I ever *felt* my soul before," she exulted, "and now all life but the soul-life is nothing to me. How purely intellectual and spiritual is the beauty of his face and head! He thinks, he talks, he writes, he looks as never did man before!"

Within a week or two, at Poe's request, Fanny began submitting poetry to the *Broadway Journal*. Her work, still a graceful trifling with such stock themes as dreaming rivulets and lovers' talk, showed no dramatic improvement, though Poe was glad to print even these things for the value of her name. One or two short pieces made him pause, however. They seemed personal invitations, not so subtly veiled, to a closer friendship with their author. As the lines of one poem declared, this need not in the least distress Mrs. Poe:

> The fair, found girl who, at your side,
> Within your soul's dear light doth live,
> Could hardly have the heart to chide
> The ray that Friendship well might give.

Fanny had not sent the invitation on a blind hope. During their meeting she had been deeply moved to see in Poe's eyes, whenever they lingered on her own, the same glint of awakening interest that she had so often glimpsed in the faces of other men. Though Poe had as yet only half admitted to himself that Fanny had indeed touched an answering chord, like everyone else he had quickly fallen victim to the disturbing shimmer of her personality. As he was later to admit in some wonderment, he found her the possessor of "a heart so radically artless as to seem abundant in art."

In the following weeks the two met at the theater, at the Astor House and at the homes of mutual friends. They especially enjoyed each other's company at the weekly literary soirees of Miss Anne Lynch, just off Washington Square at 116 Waverly Place, a three-block stroll from his own apartment on Amity Street. Here, surrounded by kindred spirits all well known to each other, Fanny would sit on a stool, her arms wrapping her knees under her voluminous skirts, her head tilted pensively, listening enraptured to Poe's inspired talk. Sometimes by request he would recite "The Raven" with all the lamps in the room turned down low. His soft voice, emphasizing the rhymes, pausing, lifting in tone, almost whispering the *Nevermore,* would have such an effect on Fanny that her eyes would fill with tears. "For hours I have listened to him," she was to write later of these as well as other more private moments, "entranced by strains of such pure and almost celestial eloquence as I have never read or heard elsewhere."

As Poe—she called him Edgar now—dropped the habitual gravity that he wore with all except his intimates, Fanny found him at times nearly as impulsive as herself, a discovery that only brought her more and more under his spell. There were moments when, for no clear reason, he held himself back, aloofly self-controlled. Then at their next meeting he would seem to have lost all reserve, pouring out his heart with a rush of fervor that left her stunned. In a private note she confessed to the effect on her of this dual mood. Edgar, she wrote, had "great self-control and no control. It

makes the blood rush to my head—a devilish power descended from the calm heavens in which I have floated of
late. He can control himself perfectly as long as he chooses
and then becomes a whirlwind."

Sometimes Fanny did wonder about Mrs. Poe, whom she
had not yet met, and about whom Poe seldom spoke. In fact,
few people in New York's literary circle knew Virginia Poe,
though it was common knowledge that she was rather shy,
with a beautiful but very pale face. It was also known that
she was quite sickly.

In the middle of June, Fanny Osgood was preparing to
leave the city for Providence, where she would spend part
of the summer with relatives. She would be away a month
or six weeks. Edgar saw her off, and at the last moment
Fanny told him some news that was both unexpected and
distressing. It was something she had heard about Edgar
from a friend—which not for a *moment* did she believe. She
thought he would want to know.

This friend said that he had heard a rumor about Poe
once being charged with committing forgery against some
member of his father's family, for the purpose of obtaining
money fraudulently. The friend who had told her this was
not a literary man, though he had friends in the newspaper
profession. She did not know what his sources were. He was
a businessman, an importer of hardware with an office on
Broad Street, at No. 13, a few doors below Wall Street. His
name was Edward Thomas. Fanny was sure that her friend
must be misinformed because he was not low or vicious, but
was a man of honor, a respected name in business.

Poe had never heard of Thomas and was perplexed to
know how a stranger coud have made such a heinous charge.
It was utterly false, he assured Fanny, and he would confront
Thomas and obtain a retraction. There must be some quite
simple explanation to the whole affair.

About an hour later Poe strode through the door at No.

13 Broad Street, where he introduced himself to the proprietor. Had Mr. Thomas made allegations against him of the crime of forgery, as their common friend, Mrs. Osgood, had informed him? If so, would Mr. Thomas care to repeat the charge to his face and be more explicit as to the time, the circumstances and the parties involved? Taken by surprise, Thomas explained that he had heard something of that nature brought up at a party one night but there had been few particulars. Thoughtlessly, he had said something to Mrs. Osgood about it, quite without malice.

Who in the group, Poe wanted to know, had made the charge originally? Uncomfortably aware that Poe was taking the whole matter far more seriously than expected—after all, weren't insults and slander almost an everyday affair in the literary circles of New York, the papers rife with such mud-slinging, and who in heaven took these things to heart? —Thomas insisted he really could not say who had brought the matter up, could not be sure just what had been said. He recalled that Parke Benjamin of the *World* had been one of those present. Would Poe allow a few days to make inquiries? He would.

A week passed without word from Thomas. It was a week that should have brought Poe a sense of fulfillment, since it saw the publication of his collected *Tales,* and in which he had begun preparation under contract of a similar volume of his poetry. Instead, he permitted himself to brood on the forgery charge, to try and imagine who could have instigated the business, to wonder whether Fanny had really dismissed it from her mind, as she said. Just how far, he wondered, had the whispers against him gone among the New York literati? Was this the beginning of a concerted effort to discredit him?

He decided to wait no longer to hear from Thomas. But he could not appear a second time in the Wall Street office. That was out of the question. Taking a sheet of paper, he wrote crisply:

> Sir: As I have not had the pleasure of hearing from you since our interview at your office, may I ask of you to state to me distinctly, whether I am to consider the charge of *forgery* urged by you against myself, in the presence of a common friend, as originating with yourself or Mr. Benjamin?

This note he entrusted to one of the few with whom he was on anything like intimate terms, Thomas Dunn English. Only twenty-five, English at that time was editor of another struggling literary magazine, *The Aristidean,* whose office on Broadway was only a short walk uptown from the *Journal.*

Poe asked English to deliver the note to Thomas in person and wait for an answer. Unless there was a full retraction of the charge, with Thomas agreeing to inform all those to whom he had mentioned it, Poe was ready to go to law. But he must have a definite name and by this time he didn't much care who it turned out to be. If Thomas failed to deliver something specific he would haul Thomas himself into court.

Poe waited in his office for English to return from Broad Street. It did not take long, but the answer was frustrating. Thomas had treated English with disdain, had refused to put his reply in writing and English's own quick temper had risen in response. The verbal reply itself only added to the confusion: Thomas had declined to talk in any detail with English, whom he regarded as an unwanted third party, had refused even to admit directly that such a charge had been made. He said that if it had been made, he could not be sure whether he had heard it from a certain other man, or had himself told it to that man, having first heard it from another person. He was still making inquiries. He would need more time, since the memories of the people involved had become cloudy regarding the discussions on the night in question. He would say nothing further.

To Poe this obfuscation seemed deliberate and pointed to only one thing: Thomas did not intend to provide any further information. By delaying, he hoped to avoid deeper in-

volvement in the business, both for himself and for whoever
had started the rumor. In that case there was only one course,
a lawsuit, but for this Poe had little relish since it would
certainly bring wide publicity, focusing on his character and
habits, and no one could predict what sudden turns a court
trial might take. Yet there was no way around it, to protect
his name he must sue.

He would need a good lawyer, one familiar with the prosecution of slander. For this, Tom English volunteered his
help, saying he had some friends who were lawyers, and to
discuss this important first step the two repaired to a saloon
across Nassau Street from the *Journal*.

After some talk, accompanied by a good deal of drink, they
settled on a close friend of English's who would probably, as
a favor, do the work at cost. The talk then turned to art and
literature and the excitable English was soon pouring praises
on his friend's short stories, just published, and on the poems
soon to appear. When at last the two rose to leave both were
quite drunk, with Poe the unsteadier, weaving from side to
side. The voluble English, declaiming wildly, paused at the
doorway as Poe stepped out on to the sidewalk. Waving his
arm with a flourish, English announced to the passersby
that *"there* stood the Shakespeare of America!" Disapprov-
ing glances were thrown in the direction of Poe who was in
the process of making an elaborate bow. Then, with a fare-
well wave to English he veered round and started walking
north on Nassau Street.

Seconds later he spotted a familiar face coming toward
him on the sidewalk. It was his old friend from Georgia,
Tom Chivers, whom he had not seen in some time, though
he had known that Chivers was in town and had been ex-
pecting a visit from him. Now with a loud exclamation he
took violent hold of Chivers's coat lapels with both hands.
"By God," he crowed thickly, "here is my old friend now.
Where are you going? Come, you must go home with me."

Chivers, embarrassed, took Poe by the arm and agreed to

accompany him. A few weeks before, the Poes had moved
from their apartment on Amity to a new place at 195 East
Broadway, a location nearer the *Journal* office. From Nassau
Street it was a stroll of ten minutes or so.

As they walked, Poe more than once careened wildly and
would have fallen had not Chivers held him up. Their progress up Nassau Street was interrupted momentarily when
Poe spotted his sometime antagonist, Lewis Gaylord Clark,
chatting with a friend on the sidewalk. Clark, editor of the
Knickerbocker, had lately annoyed Poe by some sharp comments on him in that magazine, and now Poe made straight
for him, mumbling threats of violence as he pulled away from
Chivers's restraining grasp. Belligerently, Poe demanded of
the surprised Clark what damned business he had in publishing such abuse of him. Seeing Poe's condition, Clark
feigned ignorance and bowed himself out of the way. "A
damned coward, by God!" Poe growled as he and the morti-
fied Chivers continued their erratic way uptown.

At the Chatham Street intersection Poe halted, looking
very serious through bleared eyes. "I am now going to reveal
to you the very secrets of my heart," he mumbled. "I am in
the damndest amour you ever knew a fellow to be in in all
your life, and I make no hesitation in telling you about it
as though you were my own brother. But by God, don't say
anything about it to my wife, for she is a noble creature
whom I would not hurt for all the world."

The lady in question, he went on without naming names,
was then in Providence. He had just received a letter from
her inviting him to come up for a visit. "Her husband is a
painter, always from home and a damned fool at that!" Then
he was silent again.

It took Poe two days to recover, and by that time he had
made up his mind about Providence. There was, he decided,
a quite legitimate reason for accepting Fanny's invitation.
The lawyer handling his case against Thomas had asked for
more detailed evidence, and Fanny was the principal wit-

ness. Of course, her testimony could be taken by affidavit, but a face-to-face questioning, Poe assured himself, would elicit more of pertinence. On July 2 he caught the Providence steamboat at the Battery.

Now the veil descends. No record remains of how Fanny and Poe spent their three or four days together (and there is good evidence that they *were* together, stopping at the same hotel, probably the City Hotel where Fanny is known to have stayed later in the year). Just once, however, the vail trembles. In a later poem there is an incidental reference to a midnight walk in Providence (admittedly linked to the summer of 1845), a walk beneath a full-orbed moon that dropped silvery light on the upturned faces of a thousand roses, an enchanted walk through a sweet July midnight, while "the hated world all slept."*

On the evening of July 6, Poe returned home from Providence to find unexpected good news awaiting him. The merchant Edward Thomas, prompted perhaps by advance word of the impending lawsuit, had finally managed to unravel the confusion surrounding the forgery charge. A letter from Thomas had arrived at the Poe apartment the previous evening. It carefully explained that the whole incident had been an unfortunate mistake:

> ...after repeated effort I saw the person on Friday evening last, from whom the report originated to which you referred in your call at my office. He denies it *in toto*—says he *does not know it* and never said so—and it undoubtedly arose from the misunderstanding of some word used. It gives me great pleasure to trace it, and still more to find it destitute of foundation in truth, as I thought would be the case. I have told Mr. Benjamin the result of my inquiries and shall do so to Mrs. Osgood by a very early opportunity—the only

---

*It is beside the point that this poem, the second "To Helen" is written to and about another woman, supposedly recording the upsurge of a new passion. That particular passion did not find a tongue until over three years later.

two persons who know anything of the matter, as far as I
know.

This would do, Poe concluded; he would drop the suit.
Little but unwanted notoriety would be gained by carrying
it on.

Tom English, shown Thomas's note and informed that
the suit was being called off, heatedly disagreed with that
decision. He insisted that Thomas's supposed retraction was
equivocal and insufficient, that a serious public insult had
been offered, that knowledge of the charge by this time must
have made its way far beyond the original two hearers—if
indeed there *had* been only two to begin with. English's
lawyer friend had the matter well in hand and was sure of
winning. Why not dispatch the letter back to Thomas in disdain and go on with the suit? Honor in the case demanded
nothing less than a full legal vindication.

To this Poe replied that the apology struck him as most
satisfactory, that in any case Fanny had spoken of Thomas
in a flattering manner and was sure he had not acted out of
malice. The two continued arguing, tempers rising, until
the youthful English blurted out that only a poltroon would
back down at such a point in an affair of honor. On this,
Poe abruptly ordered English out of his office. Some days
afterward, the two met again, apparently in friendly fashion,
but in English's breast the Thomas matter continued to
rankle.

Poe in any event could not occupy himself endlessly with
the Thomas slander, for immediately on returning to the
office from Providence he found that some drastic changes
had taken place in his absence. The publisher had had a
disagreement with the chief editor, Charles Briggs, who had
departed, and the publisher now wanted Poe to take over
and have full charge. Though it added a heavy burden of
editing to his own writing, with little additional money, he
accepted.

One issue of the paper—that of July 5—had already been missed because of the disagreement, an unwelcome event in the life of a weanling periodical. If another issue was not to be passed by, Poe would have to scramble to get copy in type and ready for the printing deadline on the evening of the tenth. Using some of the material that had been made up for the missed issue, throwing into the holes some of his own previously published work, getting little sleep and eating at his desk, he succeeded in bringing the issue out on time, though to his chagrin the text was disfigured by dozens of typographical errors.

In the following weeks there would be few spare moments for outside affairs. The magazine might carry only thirty-two pages but the deadline rolled around inexorably every seven days.

Since Chivers' visit, Poe hadn't touched liquor except for a small glass at lunch to clear his head for the long grind into the night. He had never fully realized the difficulties of running a small-circulation weekly, where the editorial budget was nearly nonexistent, and with precious few writers of real ability available who were willing to let their work go for little or nothing, content with the prestige of publication. He did have a backlog of his own work, published over the years, that he could throw into the hungry columns. Of course the paper made a boast of not using reprints and publishing all original material, but his own things had first seen print years ago and they were just right for the *Journal*.

Now where had he put that little poem that had come in from young Stoddard? Straight out of Keats, of course, but Stoddard knew Fanny and she felt he should be encouraged —though Stoddard had shown himself an amusing little prig when Poe had met him at Miss Lynch's: twenty years old and strutted like a peacock. Evidently, the manuscript of the poem was lost, but a word to the anxious author in the *Correspondent's Column* should bring him running: "To the

Author of the Lines on a Grecian Flute. We fear we have mislaid the poem."

For two weeks, Richard Henry Stoddard, an admirer of Poe, had waited anxiously to learn the fate of his poem. Reading the *Broadway Journal* for July 26, he spotted the notice to himself. Wasting no time, the next day, Sunday, he dropped in at Poe's house on East Broadway, the *Journal* office being closed. Poe received him cordially, introduced him to Mrs. Clemm and accepted a fresh copy of the poem. Virginia was lying asleep on a couch, the black dress and black hair emphasizing the ghostly pallor of her face. To Stoddard's quick, half-embarrassed glance the sunken eyes and chalky skin seemed to speak of hopeless illness and hovering death. She did not awaken and Stoddard stayed only a few minutes.

When he left he was elated. Poe had said the little poem would appear in the next issue! However, the next week brought the young poet only disappointment, when he again found himself addressed in the *Correspondent's Column*: "We doubt the originality of The Grecian Flute, for the reason that it is too good at some points to be so bad at others. Unless the author can reassure us, we decline it."

It was sultry noon on Monday, August 4, when Stoddard mounted the steps of Clinton Hall, on the corner of Broadway and Nassau Street, and climbed the creaking wooden stairs to the *Journal* office. Mr. Poe was out to lunch he was told. Down the stairs again to wander for an hour in City Hall Park, imagining what he would say, arranging his proofs, sweating under the intolerable blanket of heat that lay on the town, telling himself to be calm, that anger wouldn't help. Then once more up the stairs to be shown into Poe's office by the clerk.

There he was, slumped in a chair behind his desk, hair disheveled, tie askew, sleeping. Then he struggled upright, his eyes blinking in the effort to focus. When he spoke, the words were slurred, the voice husky. In no mood to be tender

or diplomatic even with a budding poet, Poe bluntly repeated his opinion that Stoddard's little verse was largely
plagiarized, a pastiche.

Stoddard, assuming a superior pose, defended himself. He
did write the poem and he was not in the habit of stealing
for his work. Any number of editors and literary men could
vouch for him. Would Poe care to consult with Mrs. Osgood?
Her word, Stoddard presumed, would mean something . . .
it was well known that Poe admired her work rather ex-
travagantly. And, incidentally, her little story, "Ida Grey,"
in the current *Graham's* was quite a compliment to Poe.*
Clever of Fanny to take a line from "The Raven" and work
it into her story: *Only that and nothing more.* But even
without the line it was easy to see . . .

Poe was rising from his chair, his face clouded with anger.
He rasped at the suddenly silent young man to get out or
be thrown out. The sneer disappeared from Stoddard's face.
As Poe advanced round the desk, he backed out the door and
went hastily down the stairs.

Fanny's story in the August *Graham's* was a compliment
all right, but Poe was beginning to wish that "Ida Grey"
had not been quite so obvious. Before he was fully aware of
the stir the story would cause among insiders, he had even
called attention to it in the *Journal* in his review of the
monthlies, describing it as "a tale of passion exceedingly well
written." In a soberer moment he had to admit that the
story was not all that well done, in fact was quite on a level
with the hundreds of other gushing love stories that, year
after year, lived and died within a month. But to say so
would be ungallant and to omit all mention of it would
hardly do. Fanny would be disappointed.

Not that the little tale said very much, or that very much
happened in it. But once the reader knew that Ida was Fanny

---

*For more on this conjecture that Stoddard mentioned "Ida Grey"
during this visit, see Notes, pp. 120–21.

herself—the description was unmistakable—and that the re-
markable-looking, but unfortunately married man who comes
so devastatingly into her life was Poe, then all the gush took
on some meaning. The childlike eagerness with which Fanny,
as the unnamed narrator, sketched the drama of their first
meeting five months before, though she gave it a different
setting, must have brought a smile of reminiscent pleasure
to his face:

> As I sat watching, in the dance, "her airy step and glorious
> eye, that glanced in tameless transport by," I saw her sud-
> denly pause—the jest died on her lip—her gaze was riveted
> for an instant on a distant part of the room—and then
> blushing deeply, and faltering some hurried excuse to her
> partner, she left the dance and took a seat by my side. There
> she remained still and pale, looking down upon the rich
> bouquet which lay in her hand upon her knee. I asked if
> she were ill. She shook her head but did not speak. About
> fifteen minutes had thus passed, when our host approached
> with a remarkable looking man, whose face once seen could
> never be forgotten, so wonderfully spiritual was its expres-
> sion. As Mr. M asked permission to introduce his friend,
> Ida raised her head—
>> Bloom to her cheek—fire to her eyes,
>> Smiles to her lip—like magic rise!
> I never saw so sudden and so lovely a change, except per-
> haps of a midsummer's afternoon, in heaven, in the midst
> of a shower, when the glorious sunlight suddenly flashes out
> through the clouds, lending them all a radiant rosy hue, and
> filling the whole atmosphere with beauty and with joy.
> Only a few formal words passed between Ida and her new
> acquaintance; but I remarked that his keen gray eyes were
> bent with singular earnestness upon her face, and though
> his manner and expressions were merely and coldly courte-
> ous, there was a peculiar *depth* in his tone, which only some
> strong emotion could have given it.

After that devastating first encounter, Fanny describes
Ida as suddenly losing her taste for the world: "From that

evening Ida Grey was seen no more in society. She shut herself up in her little study and read and wrote, and saw only
her most intimate friends. . . ." What Ida "wrote" in her seclusion is not specified, apart from a poem and some diary
entries. Extracts from the diary are given at length by Fanny
as evidence of Ida's overflowing if private passion—which in
reality, as Poe and Willis and any number of other friends
soon recognized, uncover the turbulent state of her own
secret emotions:

I have seen him at last!—him of whom I have read and heard
so much! For several days before our introduction there had
been a presentiment at my heart that stilled and awed it—
a presentiment that something was about to happen that
would affect my whole future life, here and hereafter—the
one event of that life—and when we met I was so strangely
affected that I could hardly speak. His own manner, cold
and calm, yet courteous, only added to my embarrassment.
I knew that he had heard much of me, and had sought an
introduction, and I cannot tell why, but I was foolish
enough to expect that he would meet me frankly and cordially, and that we should be friends at once. But no! he
was strangely distant.

We spoke but a few formal words, and then we parted—
parted! ah no! we shall never part again! Our souls are one
forever! Yes, cold and careless as he seems, he loves me—or
will love me! I feel it in my heart. He belongs to me, to me
alone. I do not care to see him again in this world. It is
better not, for his earthly nature is another's. He is married.
His wife, they say, is cold and does not love him. They need
not have told me this, I should have known it; for I believe
that a true, heaven-inspired love is always met by its counter-
part. If destiny had willed her to love him, he would have
loved *her*—and do I not know that he is *my* destiny? She
will find hers hereafter. No! we will not meet here anymore,
or if we do we will not reveal our souls. I can wait—for have
we not eternity before us—and here there would be so much
to alloy the poetry and beauty of our love.

Eternity! what a sense of weariness that word has always, until now, conveyed into my soul; Impious as it may seem, I could almost feel it stretch its wings and yawn in an involuntary and prophetic fit of *ennui* at the thought; for I could not conceive—since in this world I so soon weary of everything and everybody—since I had never known a pleasure which I cared to have last, and had never been contented in my life—I could not, I say, imagine how in another world I was to employ eternity so as to be happy and contented. But now I see clearly that there is indeed a heaven for me as for others.

Ah! not even eternity can be too long for *our love!* My soul has so much to say to his, and his so much for mine!—and we shall have so much to do—for, blest ourselves, we shall then feel the sweet necessity of blessing others—and so much to learn, too. He, with his wonderful, lightning intellect, which even *here* seems godlike, will *there* receive all those divine truths of which this world is but the primer, so much faster than I, that he must needs teach *me*, himself! Ah! will not that be the true luxury of heaven? To love and to learn of one who loves me!

Despite Ida's having told her diary that they would not meet again, or in any case would not "reveal our souls," they do come together again, in unspecified circumstances, and the man promptly proceeds to declare himself somewhat to Ida's anguish:

We have met again. I am grieved. I am not so happy as I was. He has written me words of almost divine passion. Ah! why did he do this? Why could not he too wait—as I would have done—with that serene and dear consciousness in my soul, that we are, not all the *world* but all *heaven* to each other? And yet it is sweet to read those thrilling words. He feels as I knew he felt—that God has sent him to me—to calm my heart—to spiritualize my being—to wean me from the world. How perfectly already he sees into my soul. He understands, he appreciates me as no one else does or can. He sees at once all my faults, all my errors, all the good, all

the beauty that is in me—and to him alone of all the world
would I wish or dare to confide the secrets of my past life
... he has generously forgiven me for all the wrong I did
him ere he came; for all that levity in my past life which was
treachery to him; and every tone of pardon and of love, and
every glance of his soul from those dark, keen, eloquent eyes,
melts more and more my heart, and makes it more and more
worthy of his own ... He bids me tell him that I love him,
as proudly as if he had a right, an unquestionable, an undoubted, a divine right to demand my love. Ah! with what
grand and simple eloquence he writes! Yet I would that he
had spared me until our spirits meet in heaven!"

It was all too much for Ida and after some six months of
moody withdrawal she joins a convent. But for Fanny's
friends and acquaintances, as well as those of Poe and all
the rest of the buzzing literati, the fictional denouement was
quite beside the point. What gave them food for delicious
conjecture of a more exact kind was the long poem with
which the story concluded. If only they had met, Ida la-
ments through a repetitive series of fifteen quatrains, when
both were young, free and rosily romantic:

> I see thy dark eyes lustrous with love's meaning,
>   I feel thy dear hand softly clasp mine own,
> Thy noble form is fondly o'er me leaning,
>   It is too much—but ah! the dream has flown!
>
> How had I poured this passionate heart's devotion
>   In voiceless rapture on thy manly breast!
> How had I hushed each sorrowful emotion,
>   Lulled by thy love to sweet untroubled rest!
>
> How had I knelt hour after hour beside thee,
>   When from thy lips the rare scholastic lore
> Fell on the soul that all but deified thee,
>   While at each pause I, childlike, prayed for more!

This, supposedly, is Ida Grey dreaming of what might
have been. To those aware of Poe's recent stay with Fanny

in Providence, however, it was taken as a rather faithful account of the hours they had enjoyed together. Before the heat of August began to abate, the leading topic of conversation at New York's literary gatherings was the manly breast and noble form of Mr. Poe fondly leaning o'er an enraptured Mrs. Osgood, with scholastic lore the last thing on the mind of either.

The Boston Lyceum would be honored, ran the invitation, to have Mr. Edgar A. Poe participate in the first lecture of the season. Would he be able on the evening of October 16 to present an original poem, to be read by himself? The Committee realized that this allowed less than two weeks to prepare, but it was thought that perhaps he might have a fitting production already in his portfolio.* A fee of fifty dollars was suggested. The evening's principal address would be given by Hon. Caleb Cushing, late U.S. Minister to China.

Two weeks—no, he couldn't possibly do it, much as he would like to make an appearance in Boston. And the publicity wouldn't hurt when it came to the sale of the *Tales* and *Poems*. But it was out of the question. He had no new poem underway, had in fact written no poetry since finishing "The Raven." All his effort had gone into writing for pay. Anyway, he had never been able to write to order or for an occasion.

He was about to decline the invitation when, in talking it over with Fanny, an idea occurred to him, an idea whose downright perversity made a powerful appeal to his antic side. Why shouldn't he and Fanny write a poem together, which he would deliver in Boston as his own? Later if they liked they could reveal its joint authorship. Fanny certainly had the time to give to it, and with her remarkable facility

---

*Poe was not aware of it, but he was the Lyceum's second or third choice, hence the shortness of the time for preparation.

two weeks should be ample. They could begin by agreeing on a subject, a treatment and a proper length. Fanny could sketch it out and Poe could work over the draft, building into the finished piece his own inimitable style. If Fanny retreated to the seclusion of Providence, she could have a completed draft by, say, October 13. Meantime Poe would work overtime to hurry preparation for various upcoming *Journal* issues, then join Fanny in Providence, say on the afternoon of the thirteenth. That would give them about three days to reach a final version, since he'd have to leave for Boston early on the afternoon of the sixteenth.

Fanny, entranced, agreed and asked what the subject might be. Poe had thought of that too. It was a topic that had fascinated him for years but which he had never tried seriously, a topic which no American poet had yet handled with success—fairyland. His first important criticism, written ten years before, had dealt with the subject—a review of "The Culprit Fay" by Joseph Rodman Drake—and his interest in it had continued ever since. He had always felt that the peopling of the American landscape with an authentic tribe of fays would greatly enrich American life and literature, as the tiny creatures had so long enriched the culture of Europe. He had already written a short sketch, "The Island of the Fay," which did manage to capture some of the mystical grace and beauty of Fairyland (in fact he had recently reprinted the sketch in the *Broadway Journal*). Perhaps he and Fanny between them could produce their country's first really popular fairy tale! This was something that had long appealed to Fanny too, and judging by her past work she was just the poet for it. The next day she left for Providence, taking copies of the Drake review and Poe's sketch to be read for inspiration. The review, especially, should come in handy because in it Poe had pointed out just how and where Drake had failed, after coming so close.

Some ten days later, on the afternoon of October 13, Poe reached Fanny's hotel in Providence and immediately sat down to peruse her scribbled manuscript. The title of the poem was "Lulin, or The Diamond Fay." It ran some 300 lines, just about the right length for a public reading. The story concerned the beautiful fay, Lulin, one of the last surviving band of her kind. In a pearl-shell boat propelled by an elfin oar she glides through the night guided by a firefly. Sadly discontented with her life, Lulin yearns vaguely to enter some vaster sphere (inevitably, Lulin was Fanny in miniature). She takes refuge on a glittering bubble, blown by a passing boy, and mounts toward the sun. The bubble bursts and Lulin's miniscule gleaming form drops to earth to be caught and saved by the petals of a heart's-ease. . . . Poe stopped reading, despondent thoughts running through his mind.

It was impossible! And the failure was in the grain— flaccid diction, limping versification, hackneyed imagery, the story itself egregiously juvenile. No amount of rewriting could salvage the work. For whatever reason, Fanny had not been able to strike the needed spark in the short time at her disposal. And in three days he was due at the Lyceum. The Boston papers had already announced his appearance!

Under this pressure, loathe to cancel the date, another, much more daring idea began to take shape. He would make the appearance, would read a poem. He would turn the whole evening into a cause célèbre, a grand hoax that would sharply focus attention on him as a poet, and would give him a memorable triumph over his Boston critics. The whole country would be laughing at the dunderheads of Frogpondium! The scheme was delicious and could not possibly fail. He would read a poem he had written and published— quite obscurely—before he was twenty, the longest of all his poems, "Al Aaraaf." It was not a very good poem, he was aware of that by now, and its obscurity at points was impenetrable, though it did have some good touches. No one in Boston, he was sure, would ever have heard of "Al Aaraaf," certainly there was no chance that anyone, having heard of it, would remember it. And in presenting it on the night of October 16 he would neglect to mention the fact of its age and origin, would allow his audience at the Lyceum to assume that it was the new poem asked for, instead of something left over from his feverish youth.

Now here was the scheme. The setting of "Al Aaraaf" was the universe of stars, with people and spirits flitting from one planet to another busying themselves about—God knows what. At this distance in time he was not at all sure what his youthful self had been trying to say, and what's more he didn't care. The action of the poem, what there was of it, was all wrapped up in a cloudy mysticism. This indefinite ness now became an advantage. It would allow his reviewers plenty of room in which to perform critical somersaults and interpretive pirouettes. Some would certainly praise him, others would just as certainly point to the poem's affinity with Transcendentalism, gleefully showing how, finally, he had succumbed to the philosophy he purported to hate. A few perhaps would dismiss the work out of hand, with a bill of particulars on its faults, showing how Poe's poetic powers had disintegrated.

Further, if he were lucky, there would be any number of commentators to detect in "Al Aaraaf" a whole raft of plagiarisms from a prodigious epic poem that was just then the rage of Boston, *Festus,* by the Englishman Philip James Bailley. Both "Al Aaraaf" and *Festus* shared the same unusual set ting, the solar system, both romped through a murky world of quasimetaphysics. The Englishman's poem was by far the longer, running no less than forty thousand lines, and it would be inevitable that some lynx-eyed critic would see "Al Aaraff" as entirely derived from the English behemoth. What a howl they would set up at catching in such blatant theft the arch-foe of plagiarists, the attacker of their own Longfellow!

And then, say a week or two after the reading at the Ly-

ceum, when all the earnest critics had had their say, the im-
perturbable Poe would calmly confess the "soft impeachment
of the hoax." In the *Broadway Journal,* of course. Oh, what
a bobbery that would kick up! The papers would be at him
and at each other for weeks, creating an embroilment to
which he would gladly lend the *Journal's* columns, whose
subscription list he envisioned as doubling and tripling in
the excitement. It was the perfect hoax! Why hadn't he
thought of it before? Why had he wasted his own time and
Fanny's on the unprofitable world of the ineffable fay?

By the evening of October 16 Poe was sitting in the lobby
of the Pavilion Hotel in Boston, awaiting the Committeemen
who would escort him to the Odeon Theater. They arrived
about six, accompanied their guest to his room to pick up
his manuscript, and spent some anxious moments as Poe
searched vainly through his luggage. Finally he located the
manuscript tucked into an extra pair of boots (in passing,
the Lyceum officials noticed that he seemed to have brought
quite a bit of clothing just for an overnight stop). Then all
left for the stroll to the theater, five blocks away.

It was about ten-thirty when Poe began reading, and after
some fifteen minutes he was halfway through. When the last
line was pronounced, he bowed to the applause and was
turning to leave the stage when the chairman stopped him.
Would he cap the evening with a recital of "The Raven"?
Now with a poem to recite which was nearly the perfect ve-
hicle for a dramatic declamation, for the next ten minutes
Poe held his listeners entranced, no sound breaking the still-
ness until the last attenuated *Nevermore!* brought renewed
enthusiastic clapping.

The evening had gone well, very well, all things considered. Now he need only lay back and allow the response
to build. Then, perhaps by the end of the month he could
explode his little bombshell.

Along with Mr. Cushing, Lyceum chairman Coffin, and
two or three others, Poe left the theater and repaired to a

nearby restaurant for a late supper. The champagne went round freely and within an hour Poe was drunk. In a talkative mood, his careful plan forgotten, he was soon regaling his companions with the fact that the poem he had presented was a deliberate imposture—yes, gentlemen, a glorious hoax! The poem had been published long ago, was in fact a very juvenile effort. Why he had written the greater part of it before he was—gentlemen, upon my honor!—not quite twelve years old! Ah, but his friends must keep his secret. He hadn't meant to tell it—not yet! There was going to be a grand literary fireworks, grand!

· When the company broke up, Poe was too drunk to notice the sour expressions on the faces of his companions as, in a morose silence, they half-carried their guest back to the Pavilion Hotel.

On the afternoon of October 21 Poe alighted from the train in New York and returned to the apartment on Amity Street, having been absent a week. He had left Boston after the lecture, probably on the morning of October 17, and had spent the intervening three days with Fanny in Providence. She was at the time staying at the City Hotel (one of her letters is so headed, in her own hand) and it is possible that Poe also took a room there, as he had roomed at the same hotel with Fanny during his July visit. The two had talked at length about the Lyceum adventure, and had worked a little on the rejected "Lulin" in an attempt to salvage it for publication.

On October 21, the day after Poe left Providence for New York, Fanny sent to *Graham's Magazine* a sixty-line ballad entitled "Caprice." In the poem, addressed to an unnamed "Cousin mine," Fanny excuses her neglect of this cousin by saying that someone else has appeared on the scene:

> 'Tis true you played on feelings lyre
> A pleasant tune or two,
> And oft beneath your minstrel fire
> The hours in music flew.

> But when a hand more skilled to sweep
>   The harp, its *soul* allures,
> Shall it in sullen silence sleep
>   Because not touched by yours?
>
> Oh! there are rapturous tunes in mine
>   That mutely pray release;
> They wait the master hand divine
>   To tune the chords—Caprice!

More specific identification of the unnamed gentleman who possessed the master-hand divine, superior for tuning chords, is not readily available. But there is one undoubted fact of considerable importance regarding these mid-October days that must be mentioned. About this time, Fanny became pregnant. Some eight-and-a-half months later, in June 1846, she would give birth to a baby girl. The child would be called Fanny Fay.

A week or two after Poe's return from Providence, Fanny also came back, and soon thereafter she paid what was probably her first, and was certainly her last, visit to the Poe apartment.

At the written invitation of Virginia, Fanny went to Amity Street where she found Poe at home, and Virginia enjoying one of her infrequent periods of improvement. Poe was working on some critical articles for the *Broadway Journal*, as well as for *Godey's*, and had already completed a lengthy piece on Fanny herself. When preparing fair copy, Poe often used long narrow lengths of blue paper, and to Fanny he now displayed several of these, rolled up.

"I am going to show you," he announced lightly, "by the difference in length of these, the different degrees of estimation in which I hold all you literary people. In each of these one of you is rolled up and fully discussed. Come, Virginia, help me!"

One by one the manuscripts were unfurled until at last there was one that "seemed interminable." Holding an end,

Virginia went to a far corner of the room while Poe went to the opposite corner with the other. "And whose lengthened sweetness long drawn out is that?" inquired Fanny.

"Hear her!" laughed Poe, "just as if her little vain heart didn't tell her it's herself!" Virginia, immensely pleased with Eddie's exquisite friend, joined in the gay laughter.

Fanny, too, after reading the critique, would have had ample reason to smile. At one stroke, the famous critic had again placed her at the head of America's female poets, in the company of Maria Brooks and Amelia Welby, and even above those two rivals in originality and range, if below them in intensity of imagination. Nor did he forget to repeat his conviction that Fanny's rise had barely begun:

> We have no poetess among us who has been so universally *popular* as Mrs. Osgood—and yet, with the exception of *The Wreath of Wild Flowers* (an English publication) this is the first collection of her poems. Our only regret is that she has not presented us, in one view, all that she has written in verse. In omitting so much, she is in danger of losing the credit to which she is so fairly entitled on the score of versatility—of variety in expression and invention. There is scarcely a form of poetical composition in which she has not made experiment, and there is not one in which she has not very creditably succeeded.
>
> Of course, then, it is a task of no little difficulty to give any *generalization* of her powers. We may say, in the beginning, however, that in no one poetical requisite is she deficient. Her negative merits are of the highest respectability. We look in vain, throughout her writings, for an offense against taste, or decorum—for a low thought—a platitude of expression—a violation of grammar—or for any of those lapses in the mere technicality of composition of which, in America, we meet so abundant examples. A happy refinement—an exquisite instinct of the pure—the delicate—the graceful—gives a charm inexpressible to everything which flows from her pen.
>
> In respect to the positive merits—to the loftier excellences of the Muse—we are constrained to speak with somewhat

more reserve. Deficient—that is to say markedly deficient—
at no point, Mrs. Osgood has, nevertheless, neither the bold
and rich imagination of Maria Brooks, nor the rhythmical
ear and glowing fervor of Mrs. Welby—but to no other
American poetess is she, even in these particulars, inferior.
A peculiar trait of her mind is its versatility and originality
of poetic invention—whether in the conception of a theme,
or in the manner and tone of its handling. A portion, or
rather a consequence of this trait, is a certain piquancy,
point, and epigrammatic terseness of phraseology, in which
she is approached only by Miss Gould. But it is in that indescribable something which, for want of a more definite
term, we are accustomed to call *grace*—that Will-o'-the-Wisp,
which in its *supreme* development may be said to involve
nearly *all* that is pure and etherial in poetry—it is in this
charm of charms—so magical because at once so shadowy and
so irresistable—that Mrs. Osgood preeminently excels. It is
in this that she has no equal among her countrywomen. It
is this rod of the enchanter which throws open to her the
road to all hearts.

After quoting five of her poems and commenting on them
in his usual minute fashion, he ends: "There is here a terse,
concentrated and sustained energy which impresses us with
a high opinion of the power of the poetess, and which war-
rants us in saying that she could do better—very far better
than she has hitherto done."* He concludes his review with

---

*Poe's blindness as to the essentially third-rate nature of Fanny's
poetry needs no comment here. Still it might be kept in mind that, as
was the custom of the time, he rendered judgment on women poets
mostly by comparing them with each other, not by applying the high
cannons invoked for male writers. And on that basis he was more nearly
correct in his opinion. More than most women writers of her time,
Fanny did possess a certain narrow technical mastery (though she had
no ear at all for the subtler harmonies), was adept at epigrammatic
phraseology and did venture on a wide range of forms. In fact it is
still possible, reading her work, to feel a little as Poe felt—that she
might have produced something of permanent value. In the end her
failure, as with so many others, was one of invincible superficiality, in
both emotion and intellect.

a promise that he will shortly, in the pages of *Godey's* magazine, resume the subject—a subject, he adds unguardedly, which is "to us a truly delightful one."

Virginia's merriment on the occasion of Fanny's visit was unfeigned, her pleasure with her husband's new friend genuine. Though she had heard some of the talk about Fanny and Poe, had read "Ida Grey," and was aware of the Providence trip, she felt no alarm or resentment. On the contrary, it made her happy to know that her husband had found a true friend, one who could enter fully into his rare thoughts and high ambitions, something she could never do herself. After nearly ten years of a marriage that should never have taken place—she could admit that now—she felt she owed him no less. She did love her husband, there was no doubt of that, worshipped him almost, but it was a special kind of love, reaching far back to a misty time in which Poe had seemed to her as much father as cousin. Such a love, she knew, made her in no way the possessor but only the possessed.

She remembered when Eddie had first come to live in the little house in Baltimore, joining the small family already crowded there. She was nine, then, and Eddie, like the others, had called her Sis. He had helped with her lessons and told exciting tales of his adventures at college and in the army and at West Point. The one thing she couldn't remember well was just how or when they had first talked about getting married. She had loved him, in her way, from the start and he had soon taken to calling her his "little wifey." At twelve she had grown markedly, with nearly a woman's form, and the three of them—Eddie and she and her mother—used to talk about what they would do in the future; used to joke about how Virginia and Eddie would be married some day. After that, it somehow came more and more to seem that it would really happen. Eddie had often said that he had had enough of wandering, that he never wanted any other home but this one.

When Poe went to Richmond to help edit the *Southern Literary Messenger,* something occurred which was never very clear in Virginia's memory. She could recall talk about an offer from relatives to take her in and care for her until she was eighteen. She could remember how this offer had brought from Eddie a fervent letter declaring his love for her, and his hope to make her his wife. He had even come rushing back to Baltimore to procure a marriage license, promising that they would be married when she reached sixteen. All of that was hazy in her mind, but what happened next she could recall quite vividly. In October 1835 all three had gone to live in Richmond with Eddie, beginning what was for her a wonderful new life. And in May 1836, when she was still three months short of her fourteenth birthday, she and Eddie were married.

Often, thinking back in later years, she had wondered about that, wondered why Eddie had married her when there were so many other girls in Richmond more suited to him, in mental ability as well as age—Eliza White, for instance, of the golden hair and pale blue eyes and the lovely voice that read so beautifully from Shakespeare. Eliza and Eddie used to talk together for hours, and at parties they would dance endlessly while people said how well they looked. Mostly, Virginia did not like to think about Eliza White, for there had been those anxious months, in the spring before her marriage, when it had seemed that Eddie might be about to forget his promise, forget how he had pleaded his love and the bond of that marriage license.

He had changed a great deal after they all moved to Richmond. As editor of the *Southern Literary Messenger* he had become famous almost overnight, gaining sudden recognition as critic, poet and story writer. Even Virginia, young as she was, could note the change in his personality—more confidence, more patience, less of that driven look in his eyes. And with that change had come his undisguised interest in

Eliza. There had even been those disturbing whispers of an impending engagement between the two.

It was Muddie who had finally brought about the promised marriage, well before the agreed date. Virginia never knew exactly how her mother managed it, since at the time she had been too ecstatic to care—a wife! Only later did she trace things back and begin to see that it must have been Muddie who somehow compelled Eddie to honor his word. He was like that, of course, a southern gentleman, romantic, chivalrous to a fault.

At first they hadn't slept together because Eddie agreed that she *was* too young to have children. He had promised Muddie he would wait two years. And they had. Eddie had even written a story about that first night of love—they were in New York then, in a little apartment on Carmine Street. In the story (about a young man who marries his much younger cousin and lives in a secluded valley with her and her mother) he described how from that night on everything was changed. Strange flowers bloomed in exotic colors, beautiful birds appeared, and from the gentle river there swelled a divine soft chorus. From that night, Eddie wrote truly, happiness had breathed over their lives.

But those blissful nights had ended all too soon—not three years, not quite three years. If only she hadn't gotten sick, how wonderful everything might have been! Perhaps they would have had children to love and work for, maybe Eddie wouldn't have drunk, those times that he did, maybe he would have been steadier.

Virginia was nineteen when she had that first attack of hemorrhaging. On five or six occasions afterward she was so sick they thought she would surely die. She would recover, enough to be up and to go shopping and help in the house a little, only to be back in bed a few months later. It wasn't long before she suspected she would never be really well again.

She could see how worried Eddie was about her, and she loved him for the strength he showed in going on with his work under the burden. She was very proud of his literary success, even though it never brought much money. She yearned to help him in his work, wished she could at least talk to him about it, but she couldn't. The whole world of literature, in which Eddie lived practically day and night—working at the office, then reading and writing almost every evening in the candlelit quiet of the sitting room—had never meant much to her. She simply could not be interested in it, could not always understand it. She did read quite a bit, stories and poems that overflowed the popular magazines, telling about tearful maidens, tender embraces and sad good-byes. They were nice stories and she couldn't help it if she liked them. Most women did.

That was why she didn't blame Eddie for staying out some-time and liking to be with literary people, and with clever women who could appreciate him. When he came home smelling of liquor and unsteady on his feet she hated it, but almost never scolded him or made a scene. With her mother's help she would put her staggering husband to bed—if she was not in bed herself. Afterwards Eddie would be ashamed and would apologize, explaining that he really hadn't drunk much, that it took only a single glass to steal away his senses.

He used to tell that to people—that one single drink could make him insane—but Virginia knew it wasn't true. Often he would take several drinks and then stop, his head still clear. It was only sometimes, when he was with old friends, or needed to escape from himself, or from the oppressive quiet of his home after he had been writing a long while, that one drink would lead him on to another and another, to oblivion and to days wasted, with work lying in an unfinished clutter on his desk.

Since their return to New York in the spring of 1844 things had been a little better about Eddie's drinking, espe-cially during the past year, and one of the reasons for that,

Virginia believed, was his friendship with Fanny Osgood. She was the only woman, of all those who flocked around, who appeared to have an influence over Eddie for good, who took a sincere interest in his personal welfare. Virginia had even gone so far as to write Fanny a note, when the gossip was at its height, expressing those sentiments, and asking that Fanny not be deterred from her friendship for Eddie. Afterwards Eddie had reported to Virginia that Fanny had set a condition for their meetings, that he must never appear in her presence if he had taken even one drink. And the prohibition had worked. Only twice in the eight or so months that Fanny and Eddie had been friends had he taken too much to drink and come home in that old disgusting way. The first time had been back in May when he went carousing with his old crony from Washington, Jesse Dow; the second was the day Tom Chivers had brought him home.

For more than half a year now there had been no drunkenness, no heavy footsteps stumbling up the dark, narrow stairway at Amity Street. And for that, Virginia was grateful, very grateful. There were times now when she was even able to hope that the ultimate miracle might happen, that in some sudden way she would get well, and that she and Eddie would become a happy family with children and a house of their own.

At twenty-four, life is never so harsh that hope may not arise and sing again, even if for the thousandth time.

2.
Region of Weir

Miss Anne Lynch, her dark hair hanging in ringlets around her delicately pert features, gazed at the faces in her drawing room. It was a brilliant assemblage, a proper way for New York's literary set to start the new year. January, 1846, had brought renewed bitter cold and heavy rain and Miss Lynch had feared that the foul weather might keep many away. But almost everyone invited had shown up.

In one corner sat the honored poet Mr. Fitzgreen Halleck, an infrequent guest at these affairs, who lent a charming sense of continuity with the past. And there was Mr. Hudson, the Shakespeare lecturer whose unique manner on the platform breathed such life into the Bard's lines, even if his delivery and accent were a trifle eccentric.

There was Hart, the sculptor, and Mr. Hunt of the hugely successful *Merchant's Magazine,* the traveler Mr. Headley, the clever Mr. Locke, Mr. Clay, Mr. Bellowes, Mr. Lester. Sprinkled around the room was the intelligence and charm of many literary ladies: Catharine Sedgewick, Mrs. Kirkland, pretty Mrs. Oakesmith. There, so young, attractive, and talented was Mrs. Elizabeth Ellet, talking with that even-tempered Mrs. Hewitt and the sharp-faced, brilliant Margaret Fuller. On a couch beside delightful Fanny Osgood sat the most impressive catch of all, the fascinating man who somehow managed to keep himself at center stage, Edgar Poe.

All those in the room were quite aware of Poe's presence and hardly knew what to talk about first concerning him. There was that awful public fight—a brawl, really—with the Lyceum people and some of the Boston papers, over what *he* laughingly called a grand hoax, but which *they* seemed to think was a base imposture. (Imagine hoaxing the Brahmins! What could he hope to gain?) And then, that riposte of his in the *Journal,* where he announced he had another poem, this one composed at the age of *seven months,* which he claimed the Bostonians couldn't *wait* to hear! No wonder the Lyceum people were getting up a vote of censure against him.

Then there was the sudden demise of his magazine, the *Broadway Journal,* only a week ago, while Poe—one heard with pity—was off on an extended drinking bout. And he had only just managed to purchase the entire ownership of the paper, borrowing money from people like Horace Greeley and Mr. Halleck.

There was also his marvelous new story in the *Democratic Review* last month, about Monsieur Valdemar, whose mind —only think of it!—was kept alive after bodily death by mesmerism. Now *could* such a thing be true? Poe was maddening in the way he avoided saying whether the story was based on fact or was just made up. It certainly seemed real, so full of actual detail. Sometimes, in the newspapers, there were accounts of animal magnetism being used as an anaesthetic in surgery, or to relieve pain, and the possibilities seemed enormous. But this Valdemar! And its horrible ending!

And of course there was all that talk about Poe's own mesmeric powers, which he never denied and which those

deep, intense eyes of his made it easy to believe. When he
stood there at one side of the darkened room, beneath a dim
wall lamp, reciting "The Raven" in that enchanting way,
one had no doubt that he could indeed cast a spell. There
was also his involvement with Fanny Osgood, of course, still
very much a current topic, more than ever in fact since word
had gotten around about their recent stay together in
Providence.

In the group around Poe, a vigorous conversation was in
progress. Margaret Fuller, giving full play to her aggressive
tendencies, had cornered a young poet concerning his knowledge of Greek, a language in which she herself was fluent.
She was deliberately pushing her advantage, and her invitation to the young man to translate some lines she quoted
was delivered with studied charm. Those standing round
could see how desperate the youthful victim was becoming.
All wished that Miss Fuller would allow him to escape. He
had brought it on himself, of course, by parading his classical
pretensions in his work, but still it was a pity. Then, before
the young man could answer, there arose the soft voice of
Mr. Poe gently questioning Miss Fuller, suggesting that there
appeared to be several things wrong with the lines as she had
given them. His tone was friendly but the listeners had to
smile at the casual way in which he had turned Miss Fuller's
trap against her. She was now occupied in admitting that
perhaps there were one or two words of which she was not
certain. And her contained manner had disappeared, leaving on her face the hint of a sneer. "The Raven has perched
upon the casque of Pallas," a woman whispered, "and
plucked all the feathers out of her cap!"

On the night of the gathering in Miss Lynch's pleasant
rooms, January 10, Fanny Osgood was some ten weeks pregnant, and was still unaware of her condition. Very shortly,
however (actually within two weeks), she would make the
discovery, and of this critical moment in her life there has

chanced to survive one quite revealing though indirect record. It is a letter, written to Fanny by a close Providence
friend, a Mrs. Brown, who visited Fanny in New York in
February. Besides showing that Fanny had lately changed
hotels, the letter reveals that she has not only been plunged
into physical distress, but is emotionally downcast as well.

> Do you know how *very, very* sad I felt when I last parted
> with you at your home in the New York Hotel? You were so
> ill, and you had assured me that you felt wretched both in
> mind and body; it grieved me to think that *you* should *ever*
> feel thus, and I did not want to leave you in this sad state;
> then I was coming far away from you, where I should not
> see you in a long, long time, and I did not say one half what
> I wished to say before leaving.... In truth I was sad, very
> sad, and when ever I thought of you after my return home
> ... there was always mingled with my thoughts a shade of
> sadness cast upon my spirit by that last interview. But your
> kind sweet note, received a few days since, has done much
> toward removing that shadow from my heart, and has im-
> parted to my thoughts of you something of that *halo,* with
> which *your* image should ever be invested. Much as I was
> pleased and gratified at receiving your note, that sweet little
> token of your kind remembrance, I was grieved to learn by
> it that you were still an invalid....

Mrs. Brown in her letter also congratulates Fanny on having her husband back with her after "the trial of a long
separation." She has just heard about Sam, she says, from a
friend on his return from New York. The rough-hewn Sam,
in days past, may not have comported well with Fanny's
exquisite fragility, but at least he knew when he was needed.
Fanny, no longer so scornful of the dull, less keenly aware
of her aerial nature, "wretched both in mind and body," was
undoubtedly glad to welcome him.

Despite Fanny's evident depression during these weeks—
the end of January and the start of February—there was one
bright spot which must have gone far toward lightening her
mood. Poe's promised continuation of his *Broadway Journal*

critique, planned to run in *Godey's,* was due in the March issue, which would be available by the last week in February. Fanny must have anticipated its appearance with some elation, for she had undoubtedly read it in manuscript, and knew that Poe's praise of her not only continued unabated, but in some points was even heightened. His comments and quotations ran to such a length that they would occupy nearly six full pages in *Godey's,* one of the most widely circulated periodicals in the country.

The opening of the review, to attentive readers, would have revealed the interesting fact that the two—the poet and her reviewer—appeared to be on terms of close friendship. "Mrs. Osgood was born a poetess *only,*" wrote Poe. "It is not in her nature to be anything else. Her personal, not less than her literary, character and existence is one perpetual poem."

At great length, he reports the success she had enjoyed while in England, giving long extracts from English journals and making it seem that Fanny Osgood was the legitimate successor to Irving and Cooper in winning the approbation of British critics. He quotes no less than eleven of her poems, and in commenting on one of her dramatic efforts, though he finds some fault with the construction, he discovers something that had escaped his notice before: "The great tragic element, passion, breathes in every line of her composition, and had she but the art, or the patience, to model or to control it, she might, if she thought proper, be eminently successful as a playwright." In concluding his remarks, he again denies her full equality with Maria Brooks and Amelia Welby, but insists:

> In fancy, as contradistinguished from imagination proper, in delicacy of taste, in refinement generally, in naiveté, in point, and, above all, in that inexpressible charm of charms, which, for want of a better term or a more sufficient analysis than at present exists, we are accustomed to designate as *grace,* she is absolutely without a rival, we think, either in our own country or in England.

Such praise, in such a place, from such a critic, must have
formed nothing less than an epoch in the history of Fanny's
ambitions, and must have helped, at least a little, to ease
her wretchedness. And her pleasure might have been trebled
had she been aware that never before in his career had Poe
poured forth, on man or woman, such an undiluted strain
of admiration.

Unfortunately, her euphoria was to have all too brief a
reign. The friendship between Fanny and Poe was now fast
verging toward a sad and permanent end.

Virginia Poe, in the last days of January 1846, somehow
came across a letter addressed to her husband in the hand-
writing of Fanny Osgood. Eddie allowed her to read all his
letters but this one, postmarked only a few days before and
already opened, she had not seen. She took it out and read
—and thereby set in motion that luckless series of events
which was to become the tragi-comedy afterwards known as
the Ellet affair. That label is misleading, however, and it
has served ever since to cloud the real nature of what took
place. The true designation should be the affair of the
Osgood letters. The difference is by no means insignificant.

The original of the letter found by Virginia no longer
exists, but from much indirect evidence its contents may be
closely surmised. In some way it revealed that Fanny was
pregnant—about three months pregnant—and that she
would soon be taking up her confinement at the home of
a relative in Providence. It expressed the hope that Edgar
would be able to visit her before she left; she so much
wanted his suggestions for a name for the child. She hoped
he would be able to visit her in Providence and she closed
by assuring him of her continued affection.

Three months before—that was late October, when Eddie
had been with Fanny in Providence. But what did that
mean? Couldn't Mr. Osgood have been there about the same
time as well? The way he traveled around for his painting,

no one could be sure where he was. That evening Virginia showed the letter to her mother. After reading it, Mrs. Clemm assured her daughter that it must mean that Fanny and Mr. Osgood had made up and they wanted Eddie to help them with a name, a real poetic name.

The next morning Mrs. Clemm left the house early, perhaps making some excuse about shopping. At 304 Broadway she turned in and climbed the stairs to the office of Tom English. Excusing herself for the sudden visit, she said that Mr. English was Eddie's close friend and for the sake of her daughter she must take him into her confidence. Virginia, who was not well, had heard some idle gossip about Eddie and Mrs. Osgood. This worried her, poor girl, and in her state of health it was not good for her to be anxious, especially about such things. Could Mr. English say anything that would set Virginia's mind at rest?

Hardly hesitating, English replied that Mrs. Clemm should pay no attention to the talk. Eddie's friendship with Mrs. Osgood was quite on a platonic level. He admired her writings and she his. By knowing and talking to Eddie, Mrs. Osgood hoped to improve herself, and Eddie believed she had a potential for the highest fame. They were literary friends, nothing more.

Unconvinced, that night Mrs. Clemm sent a note to Elizabeth Ellet, asking her to call at Amity Street. If anyone in Mrs. Osgood's circle knew anything, it would be Mrs. Ellet. Despite her youth—she was only twenty-seven—she had a sophisticated knowledge of the world, not to mention a taste for scandalous gossip, had contributed to the *Broadway Journal,* and was one of those who had lent Eddie money to buy the magazine.

Promptly the following afternoon, Mrs. Ellet appeared. Mrs. Clemm, wasting no time on subtleties, asked if Mrs. Ellet knew whether Fanny Osgood had returned to her husband. Not so far as she had heard, the woman answered. Well, then, did Mrs. Ellet know that Mrs. Osgood was going to have a baby? In surprise, after a moment Mrs. Ellet insisted that there must be a mistake. No one in the circle had heard anything of this. Whatever made Mrs. Clemm think such a thing?

Suddenly, Virginia rose, went to her husband's desk and extracted Mrs. Osgood's letter. In a thin voice she read the pertinent paragraphs aloud, then she went to the woman, handing over the sheets and pointing to the words she had just read. Mrs. Ellet's eyes traced the pages once, then again. This was the first she'd heard of Fanny's condition, she said finally. If true, it must mean that Fanny and Sam had reconciled, but she had not heard anything about that either. She would look into the matter and would be back in touch shortly. She quite understood Mrs. Clemm's concern.

Some days passed with no word from Mrs. Ellet. Then one evening Mrs. Clemm answered a knock at the door to find two unexpected callers, Anne Lynch and Margaret Fuller. Was Edgar at home? Neither woman had been at the apartment before, and the two were not only nervous but decidely sober faced.

In the lamplit parlor Poe rose from his seat to offer greetings, and he too noticed the strained looks. Virginia, hearing the women at the door, had disappeared into a bedroom.

When all were seated, Anne Lynch explained that they were there at the behest of Mrs. Osgood. They hoped that Edgar would understand the request they were about to make. Mrs. Osgood would be very grateful if Edgar would kindly return all the letters he had received from her, all those in any case which he had kept. Mrs. Osgood did not care to make the request in person, was not in a condition to do so—you will understand—and naturally she did not want to put it in writing either. Delicacy forbade them saying anything further. They had simply come to receive the letters and would carry them promptly to Mrs. Osgood.

Poe, his anger rising, insisted that he did *not* understand

and he asked why Fanny had made such a request and so suddenly.

Mrs. Osgood, one of the women explained, feared that her letters to Mr. Poe were being read by others. Particular letters.

When Poe asked just who these others might be, the women responded that one letter, especially, had been shown to Mrs. Ellet, by Mrs. Poe. A very injudicious letter, to say the least. Mrs. Ellet had described its contents as "fearful" and "haunting." Quite naturally, Mrs. Osgood now wanted to protect herself by repossessing all her letters.

Rising from his chair, Poe exploded, cursing Mrs. Ellet as an interfering busybody. She would do better, he said, to send for her *own* letters: "Tell her to look after her own letters!" Collecting himself with an effort, he crossed swiftly to the tall secretary that stood against the wall, went through the drawers extracting Fanny's letters, then shoved the small pile into a large envelope. Handing the package to Miss Lynch, he bowed and left the room.

Mrs. Clemm closed the door behind the departing women. What would happen, she asked, if they told Mrs. Ellet about Eddie's angry comment? And were her letters really so, well, flirtatious? Poe, now contrite, admitted he shouldn't have spoken as he did.* It was dishonorable. He must make amends by returning Mrs. Ellet's letters immediately, before she asked for them. At the secretary he made another quick search, then wrapped some letters in paper and addressed the package. Getting into his coat he left the apartment and walked to the corner of Broadway and Amity, where he caught the downtown omnibus. Ten minutes later he alighted at Broome Street and walked east to No. 435.

---

*For the little that is known about these letters of Mrs. Ellet to Poe, see Notes, p. 134. In my opinion they were not so openly personal as his outburst implies; it was his anger speaking.

Here he mounted the narrow steps to the heavy oak door and slipped the thin package through the polished brass letter slide, taking care not to let the hinged covering rattle.

The short note that arrived at the Poe apartment a few days after the visit of the Misses Lynch and Fuller was signed by a certain William Lummis, who identified himself as a brother of Elizabeth Ellet. It explained that since Mrs. Ellet's husband was absent in the south on business, it became the duty of Mr. Lummis to take up a matter which had come to his attention. His sister had informed him that Mr. Poe had made slanderous imputations against her, regarding some letters supposed to have been written. According to his sister's absolute statement, no such letters had ever been sent and Mr. Poe must either produce proof that they had or accept a challenge.

The mere idea of a duel over Elizabeth Ellet, aside from being laughable, was utterly repugnant to Poe. Anyway, Lummis seemed to be unaware that the letters in question had already been returned. In his reply Poe suggested that Mr. Lummis should inquire more particularly of his sister. He would find that the correspondence had already been relinquished. In any case, he had no wish and certainly no obligation to engage in a duel over such a cause. He considered the matter closed.

Promptly the next day a second note arrived from Lummis. His sister categorically denied having received any letters supposedly returned by Poe; she denied as well ever having written any, and discussion on the point was therefore at an end. If Poe would not accept a challenge, very well, but Mr. Lummis would then be under the necessity of taking satisfaction at will. Poe was warned not to go abroad in the streets unarmed.

Astonishing! The man had obviously been wrought up by his lying fiend of a sister and was bent on a street shooting in the middle of New York City in broad daylight! If the

two met outdoors, Lummis might very well introduce himself with a polite tip of the hat and then begin blasting
away. It was ridiculous, Poe concluded, but he really must
get hold of a pistol.

Tom English, he recalled, usually kept a small gun in his
office. True, he and English for the last few weeks had been
less than friendly, a little matter of an argument while both
were drunk—not for the first time, he had to admit. There
was something in English's manner that irritated him beyond
control, particularly after he, Poe, had taken drink. Still,
these disagreements always blew over and he hoped that all
was forgotten now. A few minutes later Poe was climbing
the steps at 304 Broadway.

Entering English's office he began by apologizing for their
recent clash, offering his hand as he spoke. English kept his
hand at his side. Was there something he could do?

A little embarrassed, Poe explained that he must ask a
favor. Would English let him have the use of a pistol for
a few days? He would rather not go into his reasons for
needing it. English, surprised, said that he couldn't supply
Poe with a gun without knowing what he might be a party
to, and Poe explained briefly what had occured. Lummis,
he ended, was now out hunting him through the streets.

If Poe had given the letters back, English said, then they
could not have been so compromising as Poe claimed. The
brother wanted satisfaction for slander, that was all. Why
shouldn't Poe simply admit that he had spoken in anger and
just apologize?

With this, Poe's patience ran out. He had not come to
English to discuss fine points. Could he or could he not
have the pistol?

Bristling at Poe's peremptory tone, English ordered Poe
from the office. In seconds the two men were heatedly trad-
ing insults, with English stressing Poe's unbearable arrogance and drunken disgrace.

With a sudden move Poe leaped at English, grabbing his

jacket with one hand and drawing the other back to throw a punch. English lashed out with his own fist, catching Poe on the side of the head. But Poe was on him and bore his struggling opponent backward across the room. English's fist crashed against Poe's cheek, the heavy seal ring on his finger inflicting a deep cut. Blood flowing down his face, Poe returned the blow and the two continued to grapple, swinging wildly at each other until they stumbled against a couch, fell over it and rolled on the floor, flailing away with their fists.

The noise attracted attention in the next room. The door opened; two men rushed in, and the combatants were pulled apart. Wiping away the blood, straightening his clothing, Poe stalked out. Too agitated to wait for an omnibus, he walked home, glancing suspiciously at any man who happened to pass near him.

Virginia was up when he walked in, and though he tried to hide the gash on his cheek, she saw it and saw also from his air of nervous anxiety that something very unpleasant had occurred. During the last few days she had suspected, from slight changes in his manner, that he was seriously worried about something. Now it looked very much as if there had been violence. The thought made her nerves constrict and brought the old annoying tightness settling down on her chest.

Poe shrugged off his wife's questions, but by that evening, under the prodding of both Virginia and her mother, he relented and told part of the story, omitting specific mention of Lummis' gun threat. This came out, too, however, when the appalled Virginia insisted on knowing just how Eddie had gotten that nasty cut on his face.

In great alarm, both women urged Poe to dispatch a written apology to Mrs. Ellet immediately. He must say whatever was necessary, anything, to satisfy the awful woman and her brother. Poe replied that he would not do that under any circumstances. He had returned the letters. It was enough. That beast of a woman would finally have to admit as much to her brother. Until she did so, in any case, a mere apology would be of no use. Virginia said that Eddie *must* apologize. She knew something would happen if he didn't. She couldn't stand this worry!

The next day brought further concern when Virginia began to run a fever. She had also experienced her first night sweat in months and had begun coughing again. After that, her sleep was very restless, so that Poe and her mother at night had to take turns sitting up with her. A doctor was called, and he advised taking Virginia out of the city to some more open spot, where she could have the benefit of calm surroundings and fresh air. To the doctor—John W. Francis, a literary man himself and a friend of Poe's, whose house on Bond Street was distant only a three-minute walk—the concerned husband explained the circumstances that had brought on the relapse. Dr. Francis' reply was firm: Poe must put an end to his wife's anxiety. If that meant sending a letter of apology, then the letter must be sent. The choice lay between Poe's pride and his wife's health.

That evening the letter was written. In its effort to placate the offended brother it took the only ground that could not be rejected, a position suggested by Dr. Francis. The remark attributed to him, Poe wrote, must have been the result of temporary insanity, for he could not remember making it. Lately, as a result of strain in business and family affairs, he had suffered much from nervous depression, and the visit of the Misses Lynch and Fuller had taken him by surprise. There was not the slightest bit of truth to his remark as reported. If any harm had been done, he hoped Mr. Lummis would accept his sincere apologies. Mr. Lummis was at liberty to show the letter as he thought necessary.

Dr. Francis volunteered to deliver the note himself. Perhaps by a private word he could impress Lummis with the

gravity of the matter. Late that same night Dr. Francis returned to the Poe apartment. Mr. Lummis, he reported, had
declared himself satisfied.

Subsidence of the threat to Eddie brought no dramatic
improvement in Virginia's condition. Only a wan cheerful-
ness returned—she had long ago learned the necessity for a
daily triumph of spirit over a failing body. For Poe, her
continued illness meant further nights and days of helpless
worry, a burden that twined chokingly around his daily
writing tasks, often slowing his usually swift pen to an ab-
stracted hovering.

It was in such a weary mood one morning in mid-February,
soon after the sending of the Lummis letter, that he received
an unexpectedly touching reward for his sacrifice: a valentine in halting verse from Virginia. His eyes must have
moistened as he read the pathetic plea,

> Give me a cottage for my home,
> And a rich old cypress vine,
> Removed from the world with its sin and care,
> And the tattling of many tongues.
> Love alone shall guide us when we are there,
> Love shall heal my weakened lungs . . .

The move from the city was made during the following
week, when Poe found rooms in a farmhouse overlooking the
East River, at Turtle Bay on the Manhattan shore. Taken
hurriedly after a quick search, in order to get Virginia out
of the stuffy apartment, the place was less than two miles
above Amity Street. When the weather warmed a bit, he
promised, he would find just the right kind of snug little
cottage—cypress vine and all!—further north.

Meantime the Turtle Bay farm offered a temporary re-
spite. For Poe there was the rare chance of an exhilarating
daily row on the river. He even did some fishing. For Virginia there was the companionship of the landlord's three
children, a boy and two girls, who stood, bemused, around

the couch on which lay the small, white-faced woman with the jet-black hair and the shining eyes.

Money was again a problem. The two books, especially the *Tales,* had been selling well, providing a little ready cash, and *Godey's Ladies' Magazine* in Philadelphia, as well as *Graham's,* was still taking his critical and miscellaneous pieces. But this hectic production of single reviews and articles was a nervous, tiring business, even more so with stories. His latest tale, *The Cask of Amontillado,* just finished, had left him temporarily depleted (was it Fortunato's horrified face that stared from the walled-up niche or was it perhaps a montage of female features?).

One idea for a more sustained effort he had been mulling over and he now proposed it to *Godey's.* Why not take advantage of the personal acquaintance he had made among the many writers of New York and do a short, breezy sketch on each one, supplying touches of color here and there? He could give the reader an evaluation of their relative merits, truer private opinion as opposed to the fraudulent puffing of the advertisements and collusive reviews. This in itself would be a salutary thing. Using some leeway he could easily get up a list of fifty or so men and women who might qualify. If he put half a dozen of these together each month he would have at least one assured and fairly easy assignment over the next year. He might call the series, "The Literati of New York—Some Honest Opinions at Random Respecting Their Authorial Merits, with Occasional Words of Personality." With his reputation, that should spark some interest, in particular the bit about personalities. Of course it wouldn't be necessary to go too far into the personal angle. A little of that would go a long way.

Godey, delighted with the idea, seeing its value as a circulation builder, agreed and immediately began spreading word of the impending series in New York, even using ads and placards. The new feature, he loudly predicted, would

"raise some commotion in the literary emporium." A few
New York papers joined in the publicity campaign, hailing
the sensation to come, one predicting that the famous uproar
which had attended Pope's *Dunciad* was nothing compared
to the stormy confusion of the literary elements that would
accompany Poe's effort, "with red lightning winged."

It was all a little too much, of course, and Poe had not
promised to reduce to dust *every* writer he treated. Still,
Godey did an admirable job of priming the public and when
the first instalment of "The Literati" appeared—in the May
number, available about mid-April—the edition was sold
out within a week, with many hundreds of orders from New
York, Boston, Washington and Philadelphia left unfilled. A
reprint, the first in the magazine's history, was promptly
ordered.

Readers of this first instalment, however, were disap
pointed to find in the sketches little of the promised lightning. While all were written in a sprightly manner, with
wry touches here and there, as well as detailed personal
descriptions, they were mostly in a low key. Only one came
near manhandling its subject, with Charles Briggs, the *Broadway Journal's* former editor, the unlucky victim.

Briggs, wrote Poe, was in his writings only an insipid imi-
tator of Smollett, often to the point of vulgarity. Personally
he was unprepossessing, with a sharp, thin face, narrow forehead, prominent nose and small gray eyes. His walk was
quick, nervous. He had a perfect mania for contradiction,
and it was sometimes impossible to utter an uninterrupted
sentence in his hearing. His most marked characteristic was
vaccilation of purpose. This description was nothing but a
wild caricature, and Briggs himself, a self-contained, easy-
going man, must have laughed at it. Briggs's friends, however, and many of the nervously apprehensive literati, as
well as those who on principle decried the inclusion of personal matter, did not laugh. They set up a howl.

The Knickerbocker thundered that Poe's proper place was

in the gutter, and a leading newspaper announced that Poe's
state of health rendered him not completely accountable for
his peculiarities, that his "idiosyncracies" of late had attracted attention and compassion. That sobered Poe a little.
It was the first sign that Mrs. Ellet had begun making use
of his letter of apology.

Late in May the second instalment of "The Literati" appeared, again with only faint glimpses of the promised fireworks, but with increased emphasis on personal description.
This brought from the *New York Mirror* a long article of
condemnation, in which the busy hand of Mrs. Ellet was
again discernible. The paper, referring to what it called Poe's
infirmities of mind and body, petty jealousies, quarrels, unfortunate habits and poverty, playfully informed its readers
that some of the students of a local school had "made a pil-
grimage to Bloomingdale to gaze upon the asylum where
Mr. Poe was reported to be confined, in consequence of his
immense mental efforts having turned his brain."

Then the *Mirror* went further and, using Poe's own meth-
ods, neatly impaled its exasperating foe. Supposedly offering a true portrait of the personal man, it blithely sketched
a clever grotesquerie that must have made its subject wince:

> His face is pale and rather thin; eyes gray, watery and al-
> ways dull; nose rather prominent, pointed and sharp; nos-
> trils wide; hair thin and cropped short; mouth not every well
> chiseled, nor very sweet; his tongue shows itself unpleasantly
> when he speaks earnestly, and seems too large for his mouth
> . . . chin narrow and pointed, which gives his head, upon
> the whole, a balloonish appearance . . . his walk is quick and
> jerking, sometimes waving . . . his hands are singularly small,
> resembling bird claws. . . .

Poe could hold back no longer, so he lashed out at the
most convenient target. In the third instalment of "The
Literati," out by mid-June, he took his revenge on Tom
English, who was certainly, as Poe well knew, active behind

the scenes at the *Mirror* office. He ignored the fact that English had written one of the best-known sentimental ballads of the time, "Ben Bolt," which had been set to music and had earned favor in the music halls. He would notice English only as an editor, he said, since his poetry was negligible, and in fact largely plagiarized. It was a pitiable spectacle, he went on, to see

> a man without the commonest school education busying himself in attempts to instruct mankind on topics of polite literature. . . . I make these remarks in no spirit of unkindness. Mr. English is yet young—certainly not more than thirty-five—and might, with his talent, readily improve himself at points where he is most defective. No one of any generosity would think the worse of him for getting private instruction.

This time Poe had picked on the wrong man. Within three days English, a college graduate, had written and published in two New York papers a lengthy reply that went beyond even the cleverest literary sniping. Knowing that he could not match Poe in polished vituperation, English resorted to something much more devastating, and much less gentlemanly—tale-telling.

First he charged outright that Poe had obtained money from him under false pretenses. Then he went on to recount, without naming names but in terms only slightly veiled, the facts about both the forgery charge—leaving the impression that the charge still stood—and the Ellet-Lummis affair. He could reveal a lot more, he threatened, if he had the space, and would do so if Poe desired it. He finished by roundly denouncing Poe as a drunkard, a coward, a liar, an assassin in morals, a quack in literature, a felon who had spent time in jail, and nothing less than insane on the subject of his own greatness and in his desire for literary fame.

Stunned, angered as he had seldom been, Poe began a furious scribbling and within four days had completed a

5000-word "Reply to Mr. English." Glowing from his sustained effort, he immediately sent the essay to Godey, convinced that it was a masterpiece and would become a classic
in the field of polemics. Never had he written an article, he
insisted, on which he more confidently depended for literary
reputation. Godey disagreed and, without telling Poe, quietly
sent it to a Philadelphia weekly, *The Spirit of the Times*,
where it appeared on July 10. When the paper arrived in
New York it was avidly sought by the literati, their families,
associates and friends, and all the editors, writers, journalists
and amateur scribblers of the town. How would the great
critic, with his famed skill in dispute, handle his upstart
opponent? Readers of the article could hardly believe what
they found: the utterly intemperate, almost frantic name-
calling, back-biting and nose-thumbing of a small boy.

Calling English a blackguard of the lowest order, a liar,
an animalicula with mustaches for antennae, a coward, a
baboon, saying that his foul lies oozed through filthy lips,
Poe went on to tell of the physical thrashing he had been
forced to administer to English. Then he enumerated several
other beatings English had received in Philadelphia at the
hands of some dozen various insulted gentlemen. He denied
any knowledge of the Ellet-Lummis incident (not so named,
of course), and said that on the contrary English owed *him*
money. He took up the forgery charge and refuted it by
giving the letter of Edward Thomas in full—and the truth
of *that,* he said, he proposed immediately to demonstrate in
a court of justice. English had accused Poe of being determined to "hunt him down." Now Poe took up the phrase,
commenting almost hysterically,

> Hunt him down! Is it possible that I shall ever forget the
> paroxysm of laughter which the phrase occasioned me when
> I first saw it in Mr. English's article? Hunt him down! What
> idea *can* the man attach to the term *down?* Does he really
> conceive that there exists a deeper depth of either moral or
> physical degradation than that of the hog-puddles in which

he has wallowed from his infancy? Hunt him down! By
heaven I should in the first place be under the stern necessity of hunting him *up*—from among the dock-loafers and
wharf-rats, his cronies.

Even Poe's friends had to shake their heads at such high-
pitched ranting. The king of the critics, lashing out in anger
from his throne, had fallen a long, long way.

English's "Rejoinder" to all this appeared in the *Mirror*
three days later. Very short, it stated that Poe's vulgar dia-
tribe deserved no answer, and it invited Poe, by all means,
to bring a legal prosecution, if he dared. Brief as the "Rejoinder" was, English did not forget to repeat his opinion
of Poe as a man: a drunken profligate, depraved in mind,
incapable of appreciating the feelings that motivate the man
of honor.

Even that, however, did not exhaust English's rancor. A
week later he enlisted the help of the *Mirror*'s editor, Hiram
Fuller, and together they turned out a short, surprisingly
vicious article in which Poe's most serious known failing was
freshly retailed. Poe was not named directly, but any informed reader, especially among the literati, would have
recognized the writer being castigated. The article appeared
in the *Mirror* on July 20, under the heading, "A Sad Sight,"
and must certainly have been seen by Poe:

It is melancholy enough to see a man maimed in his limbs,
or deprived by nature of his due proportions; the blind,
the deaf, the mute, the lame, the impotent are all subjects
that touch our hearts, at least all whose hearts have not been
indurated in the fiery furnace of sin; but sad, sadder, sad-
dest of all, is the poor wretch whose want of moral rectitude
has reduced his mind and person to a condition where in-
dignation for his vices, and revenge for his insults are
changed into compassion for the poor victim of himself.
When a man has sunk so low that he has lost the power to
provoke vengeance, he is the most pitiful of all pitiable ob-

Frances Sargent Osgood in a portrait done by
her husband in about 1842.

Virginia Poe in a watercolor done shortly
after her death.

Samuel Stillman Osgood, about 1850.

The Osgood daughters, Lily and May, 1851.

Mrs. Elizabeth F. Ellet

Anne C. Lynch

Margaret Fuller

Dr. John Francis

jects. A poor creature of this description called at our office
the other day, in a condition of sad, wretched imbecility,
bearing in his feeble body the evidences of evil living, and
betraying by his talk such radical obliquity of sense that
every spark of harsh feeling towards him was extinguished,
and we could not even entertain a feeling of contempt for
one who was evidently committing a suicide upon his body,
as he had already done upon his character. Unhappy man!
He was accompanied by an aged female relative, who was
going a weary round in the hot streets, following his steps
to prevent his indulging in a love of drink; but he had
eluded her watchful eye by some means, and was already far
gone in a state of inebriation. After listening awhile with
painful feelings to his profane ribaldry, he left the office
accompanied by his good genius, to whom he owed the duties
which she was discharging for him, and we muttered invol-
untarily, "Remote, unfriended, solitary, slow," etc., etc.*
And this is the poor man who has been hired by a mammon-
worshipping publisher to do execution upon the gifted,
noble-minded and pure-hearted, whose works are cherished
by their contemporaries as their dearest national treasure.
It would be unreasonable to look to such a person for a just
appreciation of the works of an upright intellect. . . .

The bare facts related by Fuller were undoubtedly true,
even if perhaps exaggerated or distorted. On some trip into
town, accompanied by Mrs. Clemm, Poe had overindulged,
barged into the *Mirror* office and told Fuller to his face
what he thought of him for his part in English's scurrilous
articles. The use that the angry Fuller made of the incident
went considerably beyond even the license of those primitive
journalistic times, yet Poe let it pass without making any
attempt to strike back in words. The reason was that he had

---

*The quotation is from Goldsmith's *Deserted Village,* and the "etc."
was intended to lead the reader's mind to the concluding phrase of the
next line, ". . . wandering Po." For more on this see Notes, p. 136.

already taken steps to retaliate on both his antagonists in court.

In inviting Poe to take legal action, English little dreamed that he would really do so. Violent literary squabbles were no new thing in the pages of New York's journals. One fought these things out in print as long as one cared, working off steam and giving the public a momentary diversion, in the process reaping a little publicity. Sometimes of course it went too far and got rather nasty. Then one simply dropped the whole thing. Authors and editors, with their shallow pockets, didn't waste time suing each other. Now it was English who had misjudged his man.

A few days after finishing his long "Reply" to English, still in a white heat of anger, Poe left Turtle Bay and went downtown to see a lawyer, Enoch Fancher, at 33 John Street. Fancher advised him that he would have a better case, and more hope of a monetary settlement, if he brought a libel suit against the *Mirror* itself, rather than English. The action would include a jury trial in a civil court, and juries were more likely to award a substantial judgment against a company than an individual. Since the *Mirror*'s proprietor—Hiram Fuller, a friend of Fanny's—also happened to be an abomination of Poe's, he readily agreed. But he made one stipulation.

If the paper chose to contest the action, its only defense would be an effort to prove the truth of English's assertions, making them no libel. In that event, no one could anticipate the twists and turns the evidence might take, and this posed some danger that the name of Fanny Osgood, entwined as it was with both the forgery charge and the Ellet affair, might be dragged into the matter. This Poe did not want under any circumstances. Fanny's name, he told Fancher, must be kept strictly out of the record, not even mentioned.

Meantime, Fanny Osgood, though she had followed the

battle between Poe and English with some apprehension, was occupied with matters of a graver sort. Her new baby, Fanny Fay, born in New York on June 28, 1846, was now some six weeks old. The child unfortunately was not in good health. The evidence indicates that Fanny Fay Osgood bore some obvious defect at birth, serious enough to make her mother indulge the sad hope that the baby would not live. All that can be known, however, aside from what is implied by the baby's death sixteen months later, is contained in two poems by Fanny, one written soon after the birth, the other shortly after the death.

In the first poem, "Fanny's First Smile," it is strongly hinted that the child from its earliest moment was suffering with some sort of severe pain or acute distress:

It came to my heart like the first gleam of morning.
    To one who has watched through a long, dreary night—
It flew to my heart, without prelude or warning,
    And wakened at once there a wordless delight.

That sweet pleading mouth, and those eyes of deep azure,
    That gazed into mine so imploringly sad,
How faint o'er them floated the light of that pleasure,
    Like sunshine o'er flowers, that the night-mist has clad!

Until that golden moment, her soft fairy features
    Had seemed like a suffering seraphs to me—
A stray child of heaven's amid earth's coarser creatures,
    Looking back for her lost home, that still she could see!

But now, in that first smile, resigning the vision,
    The soul of my loved one replies to mine own;
Thank God for that moment of sweet recognition,
    That over my heart like the morning light shone!

In the second poem, "Ashes of Roses," the implication of hopeless suffering is made more explicit, showing that the baby's eventual death was probably the result of a slow deterioration:

I prayed that God would take my child,
    I could not bear to see
The look of suffering, strange and wild,
    With which she gazed on me;
I prayed that God would take her back,
    But Ah! I did not know
What agony at last 'twould be
    To let my darling go.

She faded—faded in my arms,
    And with a faint, slow sigh,
Her fair young spirit went away.
    Ah! God! I *felt* her die!
But oh! so lightly to her form
    Death's kindly angle came,
It only seemed a zephyr passed,
    And quenched a taper's flame.
A little *flower* might so have died!
    So tranquilly she closed
Her lovely mouth, and on my breast
    Her helpless head reposed . . .

Whatever the illness might have been, it is not alluded to
in the poem's remaining lines, which express the mother's
grief at her loss, and which beg momentarily to have the
child back again. The poem concludes with Fanny wishing,
instead, that she might join her dead child:

No, no—I must not wish thee back,
    But might I go to thee!
Were there no other loved ones here,
    Who need my love and me;
I am so weary of the world,
    Its falsehood and its strife,
So weary of the wrong and ruth,
    That mar our human life!
Where *thou* art, Fanny, all is love,
    And peace and pure delight;
The soul that here must *hide* its face,
    There lives serene in right . . .

Sleepless concern over the health of her baby was not Fanny's only worry at this time. She also had to contend with other annoyances, less personally worrisome but still quite disheartening and distasteful. Mrs. Ellet's anger against Poe had not diminished with his letter of apology, it had festered and grown to the point where her calculated gossiping had become indiscriminate, doing injury to Fanny's reputation as well. Her talk, however, had quickly gotten back to Sam. Now, whenever Mrs. Ellet's name came up, he angrily and openly responded that the woman was a vicious liar, whose tattling about Poe arose out of frustration at her failure to capture the great critic's attention. He had even threatened to prosecute.

Fanny herself had been moved to write a letter of strong remonstrance to Mrs. Ellet, and this had brought from the woman a long, rambling, half-apologetic reply, in which much more is revealed between the lines than in them:

July 8, 1846

Dear Mrs. Osgood

I have this moment, on my arrival in the city, received your letter dated June 19th and deeply has it wrung my heart in convincing me how grossly you have been misrepresented and traduced. I cannot now in the least blame you for the impressions you have received against me; and I only regret deeply that my explanation had not been made, in full, sooner. It was written months ago, but I feared you would not receive it in a candid spirit and therefore destroyed it.

The letter shown me by Mrs. Poe *must have* been a forgery, and any man capable of offering to show notes he never possessed would not, I think, hesitate at such a crime. Had you seen the fearful paragraphs which Mrs. Poe first repeated and afterwards pointed out, which haunted me night and day like a terrifying spectre, you would not wonder I regarded you as I did. But her husband will not *dare* to work further mischief with the letter; nor have either of us anything to fear from the verbal calumnies of a wretch so steeped in infamy as he is now.

What is past, I truly hope and trust, can be productive of no lasting injury to you. Nothing definite *can* be known, and vague rumors will soon be forgotten. Be assured I shall preserve utter silence in future on the subject, and so will my friends; only saying, should others mention your name in connection with it, that you have been traduced wrongfully.

Most fervently do I hope you may soon forget the whole painful affair, that your health and spirits may return, and that you may be spared to a long life of usefulness, to be a blessing to your husband and children. What I have suffered, and the keen anguish of thinking how much pain I have been instrumental in causing to one of my own sex, to one whose genius and grace I have so much admired, will be a lesson never again to listen to a tale of scandal. May heaven forgive me, as you have, for having done so! No injury the falsehoods told by the Poes could inflict on me, could ever equal the harrowing bitterness of that reflection, which will leave me no peace till the effects of the occurrence (I would give years of my life had it never taken place!) are entirely obliterated.

If there be any way known to you in which I could correct false impressions or repair wrong, pray inform me by a line addressed to the care of Wm. M. Lummis, 161 Pearl Street, New York. He will forward any communication to me after I leave town (which will be in a day or two) and I need not say how gladly I would do anything you might suggest to correct error in the mind of any individual. But unless I hear from you I will say nothing, for fear of reviving what I hope will be speedily forgotten.

I have no unkind feeling toward Mr. Osgood for what he said under mistaken impressions against me. Some of the things that reached me were too terrible to repeat, but even at the time I felt sure he was not willfully wronging me, and I rest in your assurance that he will not do so, now that he knows the truth.

It is most unfortunate both for you and for me that we ever had any acquaintance with such people as the Poes, but

I trust the evil is now at an end. Heaven sends such trials as merciful warnings, let us accept and profit by them. With a full heart and sincerely can I say, dear Mrs. Osgood, may God bless you, and guard you in future from danger, and make your life a happy one!

> Sincerely yours,
> E. F. Ellet

In its way, this letter was quite a cunning performance, for it put cleverly on the record a denial of something that both parties, sender and receiver, knew only too well was true. Mrs. Ellet's suggestion that the letter shown her by Virginia was a forgery by Poe, was a shameful, woefully lame effort to extricate herself. It also offered Fanny a way out, if she cared to take it, and made subtly vicious use of the forgery episode, just a year before, involving Edward Thomas and Fanny herself. In any case, Mrs. Ellet for a while did fall silent, though not for good.* Behind the scenes she kept up her attacks on Poe, displaying his own abject letter of apology wherever she thought it would do the most damage.

Fanny must have wondered, as the "Literati" series in *Godey's* continued month by month to unroll, whether Poe intended to treat her. The first three installments—May, June, July—had presented sketches of twenty-three writers, most of whom Fanny knew personally. The list had included both William Gillespie, the young man who had made the first contact between her and Poe, and Dr. John W. Francis, two who must have been pleasantly surprised to find themselves promoted into the ranks of New York's recognized literati. In the August issue, Margaret Fuller turned up in company with five others, and was very favorably treated in a lengthy sketch that accorded her "high genius" as a prose writer. However, while Poe gave with one hand, he took away with the other. In the physical description of Miss

---

*She returned to the attack in 1849. See Notes, p. 140.

Fuller he concedes her a beautiful smile, "but the upper lip, as if impelled by the action of involuntary muscles, habitually uplifts itself, conveying the impression of a sneer."

At last in *Godey's* September issue, out by late August, it came Fanny's turn, and in a sketch of more than three pages there sounded no diminution in the praise he had lavished on her six months before. There was, however, one significant change in his customary predictions for her future:

> It may be questioned whether with more method, more industry, more definite purpose, more ambition, Mrs. Osgood would have made a more decided impression on the public mind. She might, upon the whole, have written better poems, but the chances are that she would have failed in conveying so vivid and so just an idea of her powers as poet. The warm *abandonnement* of her style—that charm which now so captivates—is but a portion and a consequence of her unworldly nature, of her disregard of mere fame; but it affords us glimpses (which we could not otherwise have obtained) of a capacity for accomplishing what she has not accomplished and in all probability never will.

Nestled in a stand of cherry trees, surrounded by lilac bushes, a flower garden and a grassy lawn, just off Kingsbridge Road in Fordham, West Farms, stood the dainty five-room cottage Poe had rented late in June. The "Literati" series besides piling up aggravation, had also brought him the money to redeem his pledge to Virginia. By the first days of July, she had been transported to the cottage, where she had promptly been put to bed in one of the two tiny, low-ceilinged rooms that occupied the second floor. The little home was woefully bare of furniture, but within a few days Muddie had everything sparkling, especially the broad plank flooring in the cramped kitchen, which she scrubbed nearly as white as flour.

As the warm summer days went by, Virginia would come outside to sit in a chair beneath the cherry trees, while Eddie struggled up among the branches to pick and throw down the ripe fruit. Often he would read to her, sitting there in the shade, and one day he surprised her by catching a bob-o-link. He made a wooden cage for it and hung it on a tree near her chair, where its twittering filled her with a peace she had not known in a long time. She could almost forget she was sick.

And then, as the summer waned, the Fordham idyl began a rapid disintegration.

Late in August, Virginia experienced her first hemorrhaging in many months. Sitting on the lawn in bright sunshine with Eddie and her mother, her gay laughter abruptly turned to a choking cough and sudden blood spilled from her lips, staining the front of her snow-white dress. Eddie took her in his arms and carried her inside. After that she remained in bed.

With the coming of autumn, Poe himself fell ill. He had not been really well since the previous winter, when overwork and vexation had worn him down. Now he took to his bed, feverish and energyless, not knowing precisely what was wrong with him. For a while Mrs. Clemm feared that he, too, had taken the consumption.

Illness to Eddie was the last thing the little family could afford. Their precarious finances depended on his steady writing, and interruption even for a few weeks could quickly drop the household to the poverty level. Through September and October, in and out of bed, he wrote almost nothing, so the full burden of care for the two invalids and for keeping the table supplied, fell on Mrs. Clemm. Borrowing wherever she could, sewing for pay, letting her neighbors know that donations of food, firewood or money would not be scorned, she just managed to hold starvation away from the stricken cottage.

The one thing she could not hold away was the unrelenting vindictiveness of Tom English and Hiram Fuller. Together, the two continued during September and October to hack steadily at Poe's reputation, ridiculing him on the score of his drinking, his habit of borrowing money from friends, his intellectual arrogance, his supposed megalomania as a critic, and—undoubtedly at the urging of Mrs. Ellet—his rumored mental breakdown. They managed to do all this with impunity by inserting satirical passages in a loosely-strung novel, written by English though published anonymously, then running serially in the *Mirror*. Concerned with the life of New York City, the novel treated such matters as political intrigue, crime and love, in the process satirizing many of the city's better known personalities. The episodes depicting Poe are rather heavy-handed—he is given the name Marmaduke Hammerhead, a sly reference to his unusually broad forehead, a feature that never ceased to fascinate English—but they must have afforded a good deal of amusement to the New York literati. The series ran regularly on the front page of the newspaper, and in general seems to have attracted wide attention. The pain it must have caused Poe, and Virginia, in the midst of all their suffering, may be guessed.

The first Poe episode takes place at a soiree held in the home of "the Misses Veryblue." Two of the guests stand apart, inspecting the others:

> "Do you see that man standing by the smiling little woman in black, engaged, by his manner, in laying down some proposition, which he conceives it would be madness to doubt, yet believes it to be known only by himself?"
>
> "Him with the broad, low, receding and deformed forehead, and a peculiar expression of conceit in his face?"
>
> "The same."
>
> "That is Marmaduke Hammerhead—a very well known writer for the sixpenny periodicals, who aspires to be a critic, but never presumes himself a gentleman. He is the author of a poem, called 'The Black Crow,' now making some stir in the literary circles."
>
> "What kind of a man is he?"

"Oh! you have nothing to do with his kind; you only want to know his character as an author."

"I beg your pardon, but you are wrong. I can form my own judgment of his authorship by his works, if I chance to read them, but before I make his personal acquaintance I must fully understand his character as a man. How stands that?"

"Oh! passable; he never gets drunk more than five days out of the seven; tells the truth sometimes by mistake; has moral courage sufficient to flog his wife, when he thinks she deserves it, and occasionally without any thought upon the subject, merely to keep his hand in; and has never, that I know of, been convicted of petit larceny. He has been horsewhipped occasionally, and has had his nose pulled so often as to considerably lengthen that prominent and necessary appendage to the human face. For the rest, an anecdote they tell of him, may give you a better idea than any portraiture of mine.

"Oh, the story, by all means."

"It appears that when Miss Gloomy was flourishing here some years since, as a writer of melo-dramas, Hammerhead was very much smitten by her charms of mind and person. So he posted one day to her lodgings, and falling upon his marrow-bones, made her a formal proffer of his hand, with his heart in it. Not having the same admiration of him that he possessed of himself, from her rather indifferent powers of perception, Miss Gloomy had the undoubted bad taste to refuse the liberal proffer, and rejected him without hesitation. After renewing again and again his important proposition, and finding his pathetic appeals to be unavailing, he rose from his knees and exclaimed in heart-rending accents, "Well, Miss Gloomy, if you won't marry me, won't you loan me ten dollars?"...*

---

*Miss Gloomy was Elizabeth Ellet, and this passage shows the kind of talk she was spreading about Poe's supposed attentions to her. It seems to be true that she did lend Poe some money, at the time he was borrowing left and right to buy the *Broadway Journal*.

The second episode appeared two weeks later and offered
an oblique reference to the sidewalk encounter with Willis
Clark in Nassau Street, an incident which had been quickly
retailed throughout the city's literary fraternity:

Marmaduke Hammerhead was making his way along Broadway, by a peculiar progression, which has been called
"worm-fence," by the vulgar, since it enables the performer
to go over a great deal of ground without making much
headway. He had an indistinct notion in his head that he
was about to do something—what, he could not tell—but
something of importance, nevertheless. That he could perform it, and admirably at that, was his firm self-conviction;
but he could not imagine what was necessary to be done.
So he staggered back and forth, swaying his body unsteadily,
and setting his hat on his head with a fierce cock, and looking daggers at every passer who dared to bestow a glance at
the disgusting object before him.

The truth is that Hammerhead was drunk—though that
was no wonder, for he was never sober over twenty-four hours
at a time, but he was in a most beastly state of intoxication.
His cups had given him a kind of courage; and though naturally the most abject poltroon in existence, he felt an irresistable inclination to fight with someone. Such a propen-
sity can always be gratified in the city of New York, which
is blessed with as pugnacious a population as any other city
in the world. True to his purpose, Hammerhead accosted
the first comer, and taking him by the button said—

"Did—did—did you ever read my review of L—L—Longfellow?"

"No!" said the one addressed—a quiet, sober-looking per-
sonage—"I daresay it's very severe, but I never read it."

"Well," said Hammerhead, "You lost a gr—gr—eat pleasure. You're an ass!"

"Oh, not quite so bad as that, surely," said the puzzled
man, endeavoring to free himself from detention.

"Yes you are, damn you!—I'll kill you!" exclaimed
Hammerhead.

The stranger saw but one course to pursue—the controversy was exciting a crowd—so he knocked Hammerhead down, and quietly went on his way.

Hammerhead lay on the pavement for a moment or so, when one of the by-standers helped him up, and, replacing his hat on his head, endeavored to lead him away. Hammerhead refused to budge—offered to fight the whole crowd, six at a time—entered into a disquisition on English metre, to the amusement of the by-standers, and finally begged someone in the crowd for God's sake to lend him sixpence. . . .

The third episode depicts a meeting of no consequence between Poe and Horace Greeley—named Satisfaction Sawdust in the novel—with Poe again drunk and borrowing money. It is in the fourth and fifth episodes that English introduces the notion of Poe's mental troubles:

The course of drunkenness pursued by Hammerhead had its effect upon his physical and mental constitution. The former began to present evidences of decay and degradation. The bloated face—blood-shotten eyes, trembling figure and attentuated frame, showed how rapidly he was sinking into a drunkard's grave; and the drivelling smile and meaningless nonsense he constantly uttered, showed the approaching wreck of his fine abilities. Although constantly watched by his near relatives, he would manage frequently to escape their control, and seeking some acquaintance from whom he could beg a few shillings, he would soon be seen staggering through the streets in a filthy state of intoxication.

At length, before this constant stimulation, the brain gave way and the mind manifested its operations through a distorted and imbecile medium. Mania-a-potu, under which he had nearly sunk, supervened, and this was succeeded by confirmed insanity, or rather monomania. He deemed himself the object of persecution on the part of the combined literati of the country, and commenced writing criticisms upon their character as writers, and their peculiarities as men. In this he gave the first inkling of his insanity, by discovering that there were over eighty eminent writers in the city of New York, when no sensible man would have dared to

assert that the whole country ever produced one-fourth of
that number, since it had commenced its existence as a na-
tion. . . . There had, most probably, been a taint of insanity
in the blood of the Hammerheads; and his acts, during the
previous part of his life, showed a tendency to the distressing
malady. . . .

Hammerhead-Poe is confined to a mental institution,
which receives a visit some time later from two of the novel's
fictional characters, Mr. and Mrs. Melton.

"We have a new man," said the assistant, "a Mr. Hammerhead, who was an author in a small way, but whose constant
intemperance has driven him mad."

"Hammerhead!" said Melton, "why I have met him. Has
he gone mad? Though, bye-the-bye, it is a matter of little
wonder. I never thought him to be very sane."

They entered the cell. Hammerhead was sitting at a table,
writing. He raised his head, and seeing Melton, recognized
him and rose.

"Ah!" said the poet, "how are you? Come to see me? I
am staying here a little while to get rid of the bustle of the
town. But I am glad to see you, really. Pleasant quarters,
these."

"Very, indeed," replied Melton, "let me present you to
Mrs. Melton—Mary, my dear, this is Mr. Hammerhead, the
celebrated writer of 'The Black Crow,' a poem—'The Hum-
bug and Other Tales,' with various popular works."

Hammerhead bowed and went on to say—"Pray take a
seat Madam. Melton, my dear fellow, I am really glad to see
you, indeed I am." Here he took Melton aside, and said con-
fidentially—"You haven't such a thing as a shilling about
you, have you? The fact is, I'm devilish hard up, till I get
some money for the article I'm writing."

Melton produced the required small coin, and Hammerhead continued—

"I'm engaged on a critique on Carlyle, and the Trans-
scendentalists. I'll read a little to you in order to show you
how I use the fellows up." Here he read in a sing-song tone

of voice—"The fact is that Mr. Carlyle is an ass—yet it is not in the calculus of probabilities why he has not discovered what the whole world long since knew. Perhaps—and for this suggestion I am indebted to the wit of my friend, M. Dupin, with whose fine powers the whole world, thanks to my friendship, are acquainted—perhaps, I say, it could not be beaten into his noodle. He is a pitiable dunderhead, with a plentiful lack of brains. . . . He is in short a gigantic watermellon. So are all his admirers. So are all his imitators, except Ralph Waldo Emerson, who, being a Yankee, may be considered a squash. . . .

"That Mr. Barlyle or Tarlyle or Farlyle—or whatever the man's name may be—is not a man of genius is undoubtedly true—although his admirers may think this heresy. I am prepared to prove that in less than ten pages of his book, I have discovered no less than one hundred and ten dashes, instead of parentheses. Can any man who uses the dash instead of the mark of parentheses, be considered a man of genius? Certainly not. The dash is a straight line, the parentheses a curved one. To admirers and lovers of beauty, the superiority of a curved line is apparent. . . . Let us, therefore, hear no more of Mr. Carlyle. We *shall* hear no more of him. I have settled that. . . . No one can withstand me. I am the great mogul of all the critics. My *ipse dixit* is law, my assertion gospel—my commandments, the whole five books of Moses, with a considerable slice of the Revelations of St. John. . . .

As the visitors leave the asylum, one of them remarks, "Why his language is very queer, to be sure—but all that he wrote before he came here was of the same character. I don't see why they confine him as a lunatic." And to this the assistant replies, "He is quite rational today, but sometimes he goes on dreadfully, and threatens to kill everyone. To be sure he is quite harmless—you have only to offer to pull his nose, he'll settle down immediately, and cry most piteously, but he makes a great noise till coersive measures are used."

The Hammerhead allusions come to a close in early November with a single sentence: "Hammerhead is still in the mad-house, writing as vigorously as ever." The novel itself proved such a hit that it was issued as a book in the Mirror Library series soon afterward.

In the little cottage at Fordham, by December, there was only enough firewood for the large fireplace in the sitting room downstairs, and there only enough to take off some of the chill. Virginia, burning with a constant low fever, was transferred to the downstairs bedroom and Eddie's old overcoat was added atop the thin blankets. Sometimes when she complained that her hands and feet were like ice, Eddie and her mother would sit by her bed for hours, Eddie chafing her hands, Mrs. Clemm at her feet.

The end was near. All three knew it, and Poe, physically weak and heavy of heart, must have reproached himself. Ten years of marriage—what had it meant for Virginia? She had been granted so little of life's comforts, so few of its pleasures. Damn that Ellet woman and her idiot brother! *That's* when it had started, *that* had been the beginning of the end for Virginia. She had said it herself, one day in a despairing mood, said that Elizabeth Ellet "had been her murderer."

At last, relief arrived and from an unexpected source. One of the minor New York literati, Mary Gove, a small, thin woman with eager eyes and an enthusiastic manner, to whom Poe had given some brief praise in the *Godey* sketches, came to call. She was appalled by what she found and afterwards, back in the city, she went immediately to a widow of her acquaintance known for her charitable work, Louise Shew. The rescue had begun. But there was a price to be paid.

On December 15 the facts of Poe's destitution became public knowledge when the *Morning Express* informed its readers that Mr. and Mrs. Poe were both dangerously ill and in dire poverty. "This is indeed a hard lot," said the paper, "and we do hope that the friends and admirers of Mr. Poe will come promptly to his assistance in his bitterest hour of need." Other New York papers published similar paragraphs, spreading the news to Boston and Philadelphia. Inevitably, the facts changed as they traveled, until one paper could announce that Poe's illness was brain fever and that the dying couple had neither money nor friends. Even the *Bostonian* wrung its hands at the impending tragedy: "Great God! Is it possible that the literary people of the Union will let poor Poe perish by starvation and lean faced beggary! Poe and his wife are both down upon a bed of misery, death and disease, with not a ducat in the world, nor a charitable hand to minister a crumb to their crying necessities!"

By this time in the Poe cottage, aside from the sickness, there had returned a measure of comfort and a feeling almost of natural life. But nothing could halt Virginia's decline.

It was near the end of January when she called her husband and her mother to her bedside. "Muddie, darling Muddie," she said softly. "You will console and take care of my poor Eddie, you will *never, never* leave him? Promise me, dear Muddie, and then I can die in peace."

On the night of Saturday, January 30, with Eddie and Muddie holding her hands, with Mrs. Shew and two or three other women standing like shadows round the bed, with the flickering firelight dancing on the dim walls, Virginia Poe closed her large, still luminous eyes and turned her ravaged countenance to the wall. A moment later she was dead.

The cherry trees were in bloom again. From the lilac bushes, from the heliotrope and mignonette in the garden, delicious odors drifted on the soft breeze through the open windows of the cottage. Now fully recovered in health, Poe sat daily in the house or outside beneath the trees, surrounded by scientific treatises, all on the single subject of cosmology. Sometimes he studied far into the night, while Mrs. Clemm sleepily trudged from the kitchen to bring him cups of steaming coffee. When he needed to impose some order on his whirling thoughts he would talk for hours while

she listened patiently, betraying no sign that she didn't understand one word in a hundred that fell from his lips. She
had heard him talk like this many times before, rhapsodizing
about the stars and the planets, their mysterious design and
man's place in it all. She knew that what he wanted in these
moods was only to see a sympathetic face. So she sat and
listened, forcing her tired brain and eyes to focus steadily
on Eddie's eager features.

After Virginia's funeral, Poe himself had become deathly
ill and had lain in bed for weeks. When he recovered he had
begun writing a little for the magazines, mostly short bits
of criticism. But he had no pressing need for money now. His
lawsuit against the *Mirror* had been tried in February while
he was ill and confined to bed. The trial had occupied only
one day, the decision had been given in his favor, awarding
damages of $225. Even after paying Fancher, there was
enough left over to keep Muddie and himself in relative
ease for six months or so.

Of course, the *Mirror* did not give up its money meekly
or with a good grace. Ten days after the court's verdict, while
Poe was still in the depths of his grief over Virginia, the
paper printed another satirical swipe at him, with emphasis
on the Ellet affair, the details again only lightly disguised.
The author this time was Charles Briggs, Poe's former
Broadway Journal colleague, who had joined the *Mirror*'s
staff while contributing to its pages a serial novel of light
comedy. The instalment for February 27, 1847, simply
dropped into the plot, concerned a literary soiree given by
"Lizzy," at her home. Poe, as the "celebrated critic, Austin
Wicks," is among the guests:

> . . . he was a small man, with a very pale, small face, which
> terminated at a narrow point in the place of a chin; the
> shape of the lower part of his face gave to his head the ap-
> pearance of a balloon . . . his eyes were heavy and watery,
> his hands small and wiry, and his motions were like those of
> an automaton. He was dressed primly, and seemed to be con-

scious of having on a clean shirt, as though it were a novelty
to him. . . .

Wicks, described as carrying himself with a "monstrously
absurd air of superiority," takes some wine, and is soon
drunk. He then proceeds to abuse the other guests in "profane and scurrilous terms," whereupon all the ladies go into
hysterics. "The company now broke up in great disorder,
and we took the drunken critic home to his boarding house,
and delivered him into the hands of his wife, who thanked
us meekly for the care we had taken of her poor husband."
(Perhaps it is preferable to think that Briggs wrote this pas
sage before Viriginia's death, and simply forgot to alter it
for publication.) Afterwards, Wicks asks Lizzy for a loan of
five dollars, and this leads Briggs into a recital of the nasty
affair of the letters. His slanting of the story in Mrs. Ellet's
favor shows where he obtained his knowledge of the details:

> The kind-hearted Lizzy was so shocked at the idea of so great
> a genius being in want of so trifling a sum, that she
> made a collection among her friends, for a man of genius
> in distress, and sent him fifty dollars, accompanied by a note
> so full of tender compassion for his misfortune, and respect
> for his genius, that any man possessed of the common feel-
> ings of humanity must have valued it more than the money.
> But Mr. Wicks had no such feelings, and with a baseness that
> only those can believe possible who have known him, he ex-
> hibited Lizzy's note to some of her acquaintances, as an evi-
> dence that she had made improper advances to him. The
> scandal had been very widely circulated, before some candid
> friend brought it to Lizzy, who, on hearing it, was thrown
> into an agony of grief and shame, which nearly deprived her
> of reason. She could not call upon her father to avenge the
> wrong that had been done her, but one of her married sisters
> having heard of it, told it to her husband, who sought for the
> cowardly slanderer, with the intention of chastising him for
> his villainy. But he had become alarmed for the consequences
> of his slanders, and had persuaded a good-natured physician

to give him a certificate to the effect that he was of unsound mind, and not responsible for his actions. Having showed this to Lizzy's brother-in-law, and signed another paper acknowledging that he had slandered her and was sorry for it, he was allowed to escape without a personal chastisement.

The identification of Wicks as Poe is not so broad as to be perfectly clear to the paper's more casual readers. But those among the literati who had gotten wind of the flying rumors about the Ellet incident, must have shaken their heads to see all the gossip about it confirmed in print—one had to wonder about this Poe, first involved with Mrs. Osgood, then mixed up in some way (of course the *whole* story hadn't been told!) with the young Mrs. Ellet, and all this with a dying wife at home! Whether Poe himself saw the issue is uncertain. If he did, he took no action, wrote nothing in reply, and let Briggs have his day. His solace, such as it was, arose from the knowledge that the *Mirror,* counting both award and court costs, was out of pocket nearly five hundred dollars.

It was in a more relaxed financial situation, with health restored and no urgent need to write for immediate pay, that Poe had started work on his ambitious and long-contemplated philosophical study of the universe, a topic that had fascinated him since boyhood. Bringing his analytical talents to bear on the puzzle not only of the origin and structure of the universe, but its future as well, delving into the abstruse theories of other men, he found welcome relief from the pain of earthly memories.

Yet he could not sever all links to the earth. Often as he studied through the silent nights he thought of Fanny. He had heard that Sam was back with her, providing financial help and protection from the scandalmongers. Whether the two were wholly reconciled he didn't know.

Strange how Fanny now reminded him so much of Virginia. He had not been quite aware before how similar was the childlike quality of the two, the bright enthusiasm of their warm eyes, the glossy black hair, the pale skin, the fragility, the simple grace. Uncannily similar, yes, but in Fanny he also had found the one thing for which he hungered most, a heart and mind that could respond fully to his own, found it and then lost it. He knew there was little chance he would ever see her again.

But he did see her again, just once more. The meeting took place in Albany in the fall of 1847, less than a year after Virginia's death, and amid all the complexities of Poe's tangled life, that encounter continues to be the single least understood incident, indeed the least examined. Somehow it has never seemed to fit reasonably into any pattern or time. All that is known of it is contained in one short paragraph written by Fanny's brother-in-law, Rev. H. F. Harrington, some forty years after the event—cold words, which imply much more than they reveal.

Fanny had been staying with his family in Albany, wrote Harrington, and on his own return from a brief trip, she had a story to tell him:

> While I had been gone Poe sought an interview with her alone in my parlor, and in passionate terms had besought her to elope with him. She described his attitude as well as reported his words—how he went down on his knees, and clasped his hands and pleaded for her consent; how she met him with mingled ridicule and reproof, appealing to his better nature, and striving to stimulate a resolution to abandon his vicious courses; and how finally, he took his leave, baffled and humiliated, if not ashamed.

Clasped hands and pleading, ridicule and reproof—has enough of fact and probability been uncovered about the relations between the two, so that the long-hidden truth behind Harrington's disdainful words may be glimpsed? Perhaps the incident really began with a letter from Fanny to Poe, the letter arriving unexpectedly at Fordham in September. The child, little Fanny Fay, was again in delicate health, the letter would have said, never having grown very strong since her birth. In fact her condition was quite worrisome, and if Edgar cared to make the trip up the Hudson someday soon, to see the child, he would be welcome.*

The next day Poe went into the city, where he caught the night steamer to Albany, and early the following morning he was standing in the parlor of the Harrington house, clasping Fanny by the hand. They talked for a while, then Fanny Fay was brought in. As Poe took the little girl on his lap he noted how thin the small body was, how large the sky-blue eyes seemed in the diminutive face. Then Fanny Fay was taken back to her room to rest. She tired easily, Fanny said, and the doctor wasn't sure what was the matter. They were watching her closely.

Poe began talking. Soon his tone took on a fervor that made Fanny recall their first days together, when Edgar's strange eloquence had often moved her to tears. He talked about loving her more than ever, needing her, wanting her and the child. Fanny's brain began to whirl as she realized that Edgar, in a rush of words, was asking her to forget Sam and marry him, insisting how happy they would be, how he would be a different man, would work only for her and the children, would never, ever touch liquor again.

Fanny tried to explain that *of course* she still loved him, but she and Sam had become reconciled and were going to make a real effort, especially for the sake of the girls. Sam had confessed that he loved and needed her, too, and she

---

*To support this critical assertion of concern over the health of Fanny Fay in September 1847, we must anticipate somewhat. It is based on two facts: a letter of Sam Osgood to Fanny, August 5, 1847, in which he says he is "delighted to hear that our dear little Fanny is better you must still be *very* careful of her," and in which he refers to "dear Fanny crying all night." Second is the fact of Fanny Fay's rather sudden death in October 1847. Together, I feel, these supply adequate basis for my conclusion above. (For Sam's letter see Notes, p. 140.)

knew now that she still loved Sam, and wouldn't Edgar *please* understand.

Fanny had been sitting on a couch, and now Poe was on his knees before her, grasping her hand, pleading insistently. But Fanny, her cheeks wet, her eyes closed, only begged that he not talk so; she belonged to Sam and the girls. Then Poe fell silent. Fanny opened her eyes and saw that he was on his feet. His face was drained of color and he was saying goodby. Then he was gone.

Back at Fordham, Poe plunged once more into his cosmological studies, blotting out the surrounding world as he spent his days and nights soaring in imagination among the stars. Here, in the reaches of outer space, all was wonder and beauty and order, here the defeated spirit could lose itself in an immensity that made earthly love, a contented fireside and the smiles of children, fade at last almost to nothingness.

About a month later, another letter arrived from Albany, this time carrying tragic news. The child, Fanny Fay was dead. She had expired on October 28, having been taken very ill a few days before.

Early in November, Fanny Fay's tiny body was transported to Boston, for burial in Mt. Auburn Cemetery. There had been time for Poe, if he had wanted, to go to Boston for the funeral. But his presence would have been awkward. Instead, under a sudden inspiration, he had busied himself working on a new poem, his first serious effort at poetry since finishing "The Raven," nearly two years before. Full of a dirgelike music, the new poem had a compelling note of incantation, as if it were a hymn of sorrow and contrition being chanted at some altar.

In shadowy terms, the lines told how Poe found himself, on a day in October during his most tragic year, in a dreamlike reverie, heartsick and deeply troubled. Bravely he tries to refresh himself by contemplation of the heavens. But scin-

tillating Venus, symbol of hope and love, continually re-
minds him of some vague, half-forgotten sin. Then it is night
and he finds himself standing in an unknown landscape before a cypress-shrouded mausoleum which bears on its front
only the single word, *Ulalume*. Shocked, he recognizes the
name of a lost loved one, a name signifying wailing and
melancholy, and he achingly remembers, but still does not
name, his sin:

> Then my heart it grew ashen and sober,
> As the leaves that were crispéd and sere,
> As the leaves that were withering and sere . . .

Behind the door of the tomb lies a "dread burden," placed
there by his own hands—the wasted body of Fanny Fay Osgood. "Ah! what demon," he cries, "hath tempted me here?"
He is in the memory-haunted precincts of conscience, "the
misty mid-region of Weir," in which hereafter he must con-
tinue to wander, unable to forget the poor, doomed child
born in sin.

He seldom visited the city now. He had neither business
there nor any real friends. When once or twice he did go in
to consult some book on cosmology at a library, he was not
able to get home without stopping for a drink. On these infrequent visits he saw no one, avoided even acquaintances in
the streets, and spent hours walking unfamiliar pavements,
half in reverie. One such visit took place on a dismal, rainy
day in early November, soon after the completion of "Ulalume." The dull, dark sidewalks and cobblestone gutters
glistened wetly under a leaden, cloud-hung sky. Passing
through Ann Street toward Broadway, he was caught by a
sudden downpour and took refuge under a skimpy awning,
where he waited shivering in the cold.

On the opposite sidewalk a passerby, a young man well
protected by a large umbrella, paused to throw a quick
glance at the dark figure huddled beneath the awning. Yes,

thought Richard Henry Stoddard, the figure was Poe, obviously trapped and waiting for the rain to cease, looking miserable. For a brief moment Stoddard thought of crossing to Poe and offering to share his umbrella. Then, abruptly, he turned and walked on.

Epilogue

Fanny never met Poe again, though she kept track of him through mutual friends.* For one year, 1848, she lived with Sam in New York City, but during 1849 she was alone again with her daughters, as Sam followed the gold rush to California. He may have gone as much for his health as in the hope of making a fortune, since there is evidence that his eyesight had been impaired.

While Sam was away, Fanny divided her residence between her New York apartment and the home of friends at Saratoga Springs. During the year she had begun to suffer from recurring illnesses, and Sam on his return was shocked to find her in what was soon recognized to be the first stages of tuberculosis. On her frail constitution the disease acted with chilling swiftness and she was soon confined entirely to her bed.

During most of 1849 Fanny had been occupied, when she felt up to it, in gathering her poems for a collected edition,

---

*Especially her Providence friend, Helen Whitman. See in Appendix A, p. 103.

at the invitation of the Philadelphia publishers Carey and
Hart. In this work she had the active assistance of Rufus
Griswold, who had been acquainted with both Fanny and
Sam for some time, and who shared Poe's high opinion of
Fanny's poetry. Just when or how Poe's old enemy came to
be on intimate terms with the Osgoods at this time does not
appear, but during 1849 he seems to have kept a fairly close
watch over Fanny, in a personal as well as literary way, probably at the behest of the absent Sam. In the dedication to
her published volume Fanny acknowledges her debt, thank-
ing Griswold for "his genius," for his "generous character,"
and for his "valuable literary counsels." She even went so
far as to write him some complimentary verses in which his
name is entwined with her own (both names are spelled
out, acrostic-fashion, a letter to a line). Griswold, of course,
was a leading literary arbiter, thus even to the last Fanny
was actively pursuing public proof of that "glorious power,"
which she so ardently felt lay within her.

While Poe and Fanny met no more, they seem to have
remained very much in each other's thoughts. As one of his
last published pieces, Poe offered another notice of her
work, in the *Southern Literary Messenger* of August 1849.
The article provided more than six full pages of the usual
panegyric, which must have pleased Fanny immensely, especially since it is probable that she had by then begun her
descent into her last illness. Most significantly, in this review, Poe resumed his former positive feelings about her
promising future: "Upon the whole, I have spoken of Mrs.
Osgood so much in detail, less on account of what she has
actually done than on account of what I perceive in her the
ability to do." For his moment of anger in the "Literati"
piece, he had made amends.

On Fanny's part, soon after she received the shocking news
of Poe's sudden death in Baltimore on October 7, 1849, she
composed at least two poems in his memory, and later she
supplied Griswold with a brief but revealing memoir, for

inclusion in his first brief biography of Poe (*International Miscellany*, May 1850, later printed in the first volume of Poe's *Works*). Neither poem mentions Poe by name, but there is no doubt of whom they speak. The first, "I Cannot Forget Him," is surprisingly unguarded:

> I cannot forget him! I've locked up my soul;
> But not till his image deep, deep in it stole . . .
>
> I turn to my books, but his voice, rich and rare,
> Is blent with the genius that speaks to me there.
>
> I tune my wild lyre; but I think of the praise,
> Too precious, too dear, that he lent to my lays . . .
>
> He haunts me forever, I worship him yet;
> O! idle endeavor, I cannot forget!

The second poem manages to speak more reticently, but it still reveals the permanent place that his genius and memory had found in her heart:

> The hand that swept the sounding lyre
>   With more than mortal skill,
> The lightning eye, the heart of fire,
>   The fervent lip are still;
> No more in rapture or in wo
>   With melody to thrill,
>   Ah, nevermore!
>
> Love's silver lyre he played so well
>   Lies shattered on his tomb;
> But still in air its music spell
>   Floats on through light and gloom,
> And in the hearts where soft they fell
>   His words of beauty bloom
>   For evermore!

Her memoir of Poe, written probably in March 1850, is brief, to the point, and amounts to little more than a not-so-subtle defense of herself against all the gossip that still pursued her. It opens:

You ask me, my friend, to write for you my reminiscences of Edgar Poe. For you, who knew and understood my affectionate interest in him, and my frank acknowledgment of that interest to all who had a claim upon my confidence, for you, I will willingly do so. I think no one could know him —no one *has* known him personally—certainly no woman— without feeling the same interest. I can sincerely say that, although I have frequently *heard* of abberations on his part from "the straight and narrow path," I have never *seen* him otherwise than gentle, generous, well-bred and fastidiously refined. To a sensitive and delicately nurtured woman, there was a peculiar and irresistable charm in the chivalric, graceful and almost tender reverence with which he invariably approached all women who won his respect. It was this which first commanded and always retained my regard for him.

I have been told that when his sorrows and pecuniary embarrassments had driven him to the use of stimulants, which a less delicate organization might have borne without injury, he was in the habit of speaking disrespectfully of the ladies of his acquaintance. It is difficult for me to believe this; for to me, to whom he came during the year of our acquaintance, for counsel and kindness in all his many anxieties and griefs, he never spoke irreverently of any woman save one, and then only in *my* defense; and though I rebuked him for his momentary forgetfulness of the respect due to himself and to me, I could not but forgive the offense for the sake of the generous impulse which prompted it.

Yet even were these sad rumors true of him, the wise and well-informed knew how to regard, as they would the impetuous anger of a spoiled infant balked of its capricious will, the equally harmless and unmeaning phrensy of that stray child of Poetry and Passion. For the few unwomanly and slander-loving gossips who have injured *him* and *themselves* only, by repeating his ravings, when in such moods they have accepted his society, I have only to vouchsafe my wonder and my pity. They cannot surely harm the true and pure, who, reverencing his genius and pitying his misfortunes and his errors, endeavored by their timely kindness and sympathy to soothe his sad career....

Fanny herself, of course, was the "true and pure" friend meant to be inferred by that last sentence. The remainder of the sketch carefully concentrates on Poe's evidently happy home life, and his apparently idylic marriage with Virginia, "the only woman whom he ever truly loved." This is a point that Fanny feels it urgent to stress, managing in the process to raise doubts even in the casual reader:

> Of the charming love and confidence that existed between his wife and himself, always delightfully apparent to me, in spite of the many little poetical episodes, in which the impassioned romance of his temperament impelled him to indulge; of this I cannot speak too earnestly—too warmly.

She ends her sketch with a reference to what must have been a fairly regular correspondence between them: "It was in his conversations and his letters, far more than in his published poetry and prose writings, that the genius of Poe was most gloriously revealed. His letters were divinely beautiful. . . ." Those letters, like Fanny's to him, were long ago carefully and completely destroyed—his no doubt by Sam, hers certainly by Mrs. Clemm, who further records the interesting fact that at some point Griswold offered her the large sum of $500 for them.

Within about three months of Sam's return from California, by early May, Fanny's condition had deteriorated to the point where her physician, her family and friends all recognized that she was nearing the end. For some reason, Sam chose this moment to move his family to a new apartment at 112 West Twenty-Second Street, and Fanny, caught up in the excitement of selecting fabric for new drapes and furniture, the samples brought to her bedside, repeatedly exclaimed to her husband and to the few visitors she was allowed, "We shall be so happy!" All could see, however, that her life was ebbing fast and it was finally determined to tell her so. The sad task was delegated to Griswold, who later recalled:

I wrote the terrible truth to her, in studiously gentle words, reminding her that in heaven there is richer and more delicious beauty . . . and that they know not any sorrow who are with Our Father. She read the brief note almost to the end silently, and then turned upon her pillow like a child and wept. "I cannot leave my beautiful home," she said, looking about upon the souvenirs of many an affectionate recollection, "and my noble husband and Lily and May." But the sentence was confirmed by other friends and she resigned herself to the will of God.

Five days before her death Fanny wrote her last poem, a thank-you to a young girl who had made paper roses for her. To the end, her art was autobiographical, as the final stanza of that last poem so mournfully shows:

> I'm going through the eternal gates
> Ere June's sweet roses blow;
> Death's lovely angel leads me there
> And it is sweet to go.

On the afternoon of Sunday, May 12, 1850, suffering little or no pain, she died. Thereafter, her unique personality remained in the hearts of her friends as a bright warm glow. Not a few of them seriously felt that, in knowing her, they had been in touch with primal innocence. Soon, plans were made to issue a memorial volume in her honor, offering selections of poetry and prose from those who had loved her. The volume, edited by Fanny's close friend, Mrs. Hewitt, appeared in 1851, with a proud list of contributors. Included were Richard Henry Stoddard and Rufus Griswold, the two who were to initiate, and sustain for so long, that bitter campaign against Poe's reputation.

Griswold's role in all of this, with his *Tribune* obituary and his *Memoir*, needs no rehearsal—though it may now be easier to understand why in the *Tribune* he wrote so cruelly that "few will be grieved" by the announcement of Poe's death because the poet "had few or no friends." But the offended Stoddard, it is not always remembered, played almost as crucial a part in the denigration as did Griswold. It might be argued, in fact, that Stoddard did the greater damage. His eventual rise to the literary heights, as editor and author, supplied him with a national platform for his opinions, public and private, over many decades, and his abhorence of Poe never slackened. His attacks began some three years after Poe's death, in the *National Magazine,* March 1853, where he emphasizes Poe's drunkenness and says that he had no real heart, no conscience, no morality. Nearly forty years later, in *Lippincott's Magazine,* March 1889, he still nurtures a sense of outrage, writing vulgarly and without explanation of Poe as "this needy poet with two sickly women on his lap." Few if any of Stoddard's readers at that late date could have guessed that this odd sentence referred to Virginia and Fanny, harking back to matters that had by then lain in darkness for nearly half a century. Death, for any other man, might have cancelled the memory of many human failings. But for Poe, because of what he had done to Fanny, there was to be no forgiveness.

In Poe's defense, at first, only a few strong voices were raised, particularly those of George Graham and Helen Whitman, both of whom had known Fanny almost as well as they had known Poe. Thus the controversy over Poe's character continued down the years, with both sides always taking care never to name its underlying cause, its real cause. The beloved Mrs. Osgood, her reputation reclaimed, was to be allowed to rest in peace, and little Fanny Fay in silence and oblivion.

Appendix A

The Oil Portrait of Poe by S. S. Osgood

There is in existence a bust portrait of Poe, about half life size, done in oils by Sam Osgood, Fanny's husband. Now the property of the New York Historical Society, the picture has often been reproduced and is quite familiar to students of Poe. Its date is always given as 1845, and this has been looked on as proof, in some sort, that there could have been nothing questionable in the friendship of Fanny and Poe— the husband, it is said, would hardly have immortalized the features of even a suspected rival. A niece of Osgood, in fact, made just this claim: "I know well that there would never have existed a portrait of the poet from my uncle's brush if there had not been a kindly feeling between them." (Phillips, p. 997). While the portrait would not, by itself and whenever it was done, disprove a liaison between Fanny and Poe, some explanation of its existence is needed.

It develops that the year 1845 for the painting's execution does not rest on documentary evidence of any sort, neither indirectly nor in any way by implication. The records of the

The Whitman daguerreotype.

Oil portrait of Poe by Sam Osgood.

Watercolor of Poe from *Graham's* magazine.

Historical Society have nothing whatever to say on the point, nor does the portrait receive mention in contemporary records—memoirs, biographies, letters published and unpublished, lists of art exhibits—that I have studied. Poe's own letters for 1845 (some thirty-seven are printed by Ostrom) say nothing about a painting, nor do those of 1846-49. The portrait itself, (which I examined at the Historical Society) carries neither date nor signature. Just when and how the year 1845 became attached to the painting I have not been able to discover, but it was probably about the turn of the century (and I suspect that the claim was first put forward by Osgood's relatives).

If the year of composition was not 1845 then it becomes difficult to account for the painting at all. Since Sam Osgood was absent in California from February 5, 1849 until after Poe's death, it must have been done in the three-year period 1846-48. But there is no record of Poe sitting to an artist, any artist, during that time. In addition, after January 1846 Poe's association with Mrs. Osgood was ended.

The only reference of any sort to the portrait during Poe's lifetime, so far as I can find, was that recalled long afterward by John Sartain (*Lippincott's,* March 1889). He reports an incidental mention of it by Poe himself in Philadelphia in the summer of 1849: drinking heavily and very troubled about his affairs, Poe asked Sartain, in the event of his death, to promise that he would get the portrait and give it to Mrs. Clemm (that is the whole extent of the mention). If nothing else, the reference does at least establish that the picture was done while Poe was alive, though not indicating the year. There are a few *later* references, however, which begin to suggest an answer to the puzzle.

Early in 1850, some months after Poe's death, the portrait passed into the possession of Rufus Griswold, who had it engraved as frontispiece for the first volume of Poe's *Works,* which Griswold had edited. A line underneath this frontispiece reads:"Engraved by J. Sartain from the original pic-

ture in the collection of R. W. Griswold." (Sartain's involvement with the painting at this point had nothing to do with
Poe's request of the previous summer, but was due to Sartain's position as one of the country's leading engravers.)
Ordinarily, of course, the name of the original artist would
also appear in the credit line, but Osgood's name in this instance is conspicuously missing.

By 1856 Griswold was in financial straits, and in order to
preserve his art collection he had it transferred to the home
of a friend in Brooklyn, Alice Cary. Included were a portrait of Fanny Osgood by her husband, one of Griswold by
Elliot, and the Osgood Poe. In Miss Cary's home these three
were hung in a curtained niche with special lighting. Here
they were reverently viewed shortly afterward by none other
than Helen Whitman, a friend of Miss Cary. When in 1857
Griswold died suddenly, Mrs. Whitman promptly inquired
of a friend, "'What became of the other portraits, Mrs. Osgood's and Edgar Poe's?" (Ticknor, p. 183).

Griswold, a member of the New York Historical Society,
left his entire art collection to that body along with the bulk
of his literary papers. Today the Society's records show that
transfer of the papers did not take place until 1864. There
is no record of just when the portrait itself was transferred.
(In fact the Society's records have no mention of the portrait whatever.)

Mrs. Whitman's only other reference to the portrait occurs in her 1860 defense of Poe, in which she criticizes the
Sartain engraving of the Osgood portrait as very unlike him
(which it certainly is). She also dismisses the face in the
original painting as having a "cold, automatic look." And
in that observation by one who knew Poe well in life, and
who had studied the portrait closely, I believe lies the key
to the painting's secret. It was not done from life at all, but
copied from a daguerreotype, in November-December 1848.

Poe's connection with Helen Whitman began in September 1848. After a troubled whirlwind courtship, the two be-

came engaged on November 13 of that year, and there ensued a calm period of about a month in which Poe and his Helen prepared for marriage. During this time, Fanny Osgood, an old friend of Mrs. Whitman, paid a visit to Providence and called to offer congratulations (Winwar, p. 347, and Miller, *Biography*, p. 218). What else may have transpired between these two at this visit is unknown, except that at one point Fanny asked Mrs. Whitman to convey a message to Poe, a message that made Mrs. Whitman feel uneasy. It was during this visit, I believe, that Fanny also offered to have Sam do a portrait of Poe as a wedding gift.

The most striking fact about the Osgood-Poe portrait is that it does not look much like its subject, in fact very unlike. It is also what Mrs. Whitman called it, cold and automatic, quite obviously an idealization. And yet it does bear a close, general resemblance—even to the stray lock of hair over the right eye—to a daguerreotype of Poe made in Providence on November 14, 1848, and presented by Poe to Mrs. Whitman (the so-called "Whitman daguerreotype;" (See frontispiece). If Osgood did work from this daguerreotype, he may also have had at hand a copy of an earlier portrait engraving of Poe which had appeared in *Graham's* for February 1845. Definite elements of this *Graham's* engraving, a very poor one, are suggested by Osgood's painting. (See the accompanying illustrations for a comparison of all three pictures.)

The only strong objection to this theory is the absence of a moustache in the Osgood portrait, while in the 1848 daguerreotype, a moustache is present (there is none in the *Graham's* engraving). But the objection is not a serious one. It is known that when Fanny was meeting Poe in 1845 he did not wear a moustache. It is likely that Fanny persuaded Mrs. Whitman to have the oil portrait depict a clean-shaven Poe as nobler and more youthful.

Poe's engagement to Mrs. Whitman, after a month or so of calm, came to a sudden end just before Christmas 1848.

Since there was to be no marriage, the portrait was no longer appropriate as a gift, and perhaps it was not quite finished at the time. Then, a year later, Poe was dead, and Griswold soon after began the preparation of Poe's *Collected Works* —just at the time when he was a frequent visitor at the new Osgood apartment (112 West Twenty-Second Street, New York City) where Fanny was in the final stages of her illness. Whether Griswold bought the picture or received it as a gift, was there perhaps a prohibition by Sam that the name of the artist should not accompany its reproduction in Poe's *Works*?

(Sources for the above discussion: Didier, E., *The Poe Cult and Other Papers*; Phillips, M., *EAP The Man*; Sartain, J., "Reminiscences of EAP," *Lippincott's* March 1889; Sartain, J., *Reminiscences of a Very Old Man*; Schulte, A., *Facts About Poe, Illustrated*; Ticknor, C., *Poe's Helen*; Whitman, H., *Edgar Poe and His Critics*; Winwar, F., *The Haunted Palace*. I have also consulted the biographies by Gill, Weiss, Ingram, Woodberry, Harrison, Allen, and Quinn.)

Appendix B

"Lulin, or The Diamond Fay,"
by Frances S. Osgood

It does no good to Fanny Osgood's literary reputation, tenuous enough as it is, to reprint this occasional poem for a modern audience. It would have been much better to allow it to molder away in the pages of Sartain's *Union Magazine*, where it appeared 132 years ago, in May and July 1848 (note, not June but *July*, and there is no explanation of why a month was skipped in giving the second part). It was reprinted in Fanny's *Works*, 1850, of which Rufus Griswold was editor, but only for its role in the relations between Fanny and Poe do I resurrect it here.

All that is known, directly, about this poem, and its link to Poe, comes from Griswold, who had his information from Fanny herself. In his *Memoir* of Poe he writes:

When he accepted the invitation of the Lyceum he intended to write an original poem, upon a subject which he said had haunted his imagination for years; but cares, anxiety, and

feebleness of will prevented; and a week before the appointed
night he wrote to a friend, imploring assistance. "You compose with such astonishing facility," he urged in his letter,
"that you can easily furnish me, quite soon enough, a
poem that will be equal to my reputation. For the love of
God I beseech you to help me in this extremity." The lady
wrote him kindly, advising him judiciously, but promising
to attempt the fulfillment of his wishes. She was, however, an
invalid, and so failed.

To that statement Griswold adds a footnote: "This lady was
the late Mrs. Osgood, and a fragment of what she wrote
under these circumstances may be found in the last edition
of her works under the title of 'Lulin, or The Diamond
Fay.'" Fanny in 1845 was not an invalid, of course; that is
just Griswold's way of excusing her failure.

Regarding that sentence quoted from a supposed letter of
Poe to Fanny, let the reader beware, since it may be another
deft bit of forgery, to make Poe engage in outright pleading,
and make Fanny's compliance seem reluctant (the *Memoir,*
as is well known, contains other forgeries; see Quinn, pp.
668-72). If Griswold did not wholly invent the letter and
the quote he makes from it, he certainly would not have
hesitated to alter an actual letter. My own opinion is that
Fanny simply *told* Griswold about such a letter, and para-
phrased the request from Poe, leaving Griswold with plenty
of room for interpretation.

That Poe helped Fanny to rework the poem for publication, during his stopover at Providence in October 1845 as
he returned from Boston, is of course only a guess on my part.
But I think I can see traces of his hand in lines 74-97, especially in the use of parentheses at lines 85-87, and in the structure and tone of those parenthetical lines. I give the poem
exactly as it appeared in the *Union Magazine,* not even spar-
ing its heavy rain of dashes. "Part First" appeared in the May
issue, "Part II" (sic) in July.

Lulin, or The Diamond Fay.
A Fairy Legend;
Sent by a lover to his mistress, with a diamond ring.
by Frances S. Osgood

Part First

Fair Lilith, listen, while I sing,
  The legend of this diamond ring,
And in its moral, maiden, heed
  A quiet 'hint your heart may need.'
In fairy archives, where 'tis told,
  I found the story quaint and old,
Writ on a richly-blazoned page
  Of parchment, by some elfin sage.

Long was the night to Lulin!—Discontent
With dew and flowers,—with fairy dance and song,—
Her pearl-shell boat upon the little stream,
Lit by a firefly, which her spells transfixed,
And lined with a warm blush some flower had given,
Where she was wont to lie and furl at will
The lily-leaf and ply her elfin oar,—
Her white moth-courser, harnessed with gold hair,—
Her tiny, silver-chorded lute, on which
She played the violet's lullaby, until
It bent in balmy slumber,—all were vain,
All wearied her.—Vague yearnings for a sphere
more high and vast had filled her ardent soul.
And once, at dawn, when soft the signal rang,
That every morning warned the dainty troop,
On pain of death to fly the approach of Day,
Our wilful Lulin lingered!—but an instant—
Yet in that instant she was seen and loved,
And loved again,—Alas! the first, rich ray,
The glorious herald of the coming morn,
Lit on the greensward at her very feet!
She fled in fear, yet with a rapturous thrill
At heart that haunted her.—And now she lay

Upon her rose-leaf couch,—half wild with doubt
And hope,—when lo! just ere the dawn,
A bubble, blown by some blithe cottage imp,
Floated above her! Like a gleam of light,
Up glided Lulin from her fragrant bed,
And clapped her delicate hands and cried "For me!
For me—the strange balloon! 'Tis bound to Heaven!
Thus when I leave the cares of life forever,
And meet my love!" She plumed her luminous wings;
She flew to mount the slowly soaring orb,
And, poised upon it—proudly looked below!
Ah, heaven, what warm embrace enfolds her form?
Her sunlit god alights beside her there!
And the car, suddenly illumined, glows
Beneath the glory of his smile; and up
They sail exulting in their joy;—but hark!
The signal sounds! The musical fairy gong!
Once—twice—ah fate! ere thrice its tones resound,
The fragile bubble breaks! Alas for Lulin!
Down from her dizzy height, in sight of all,
Of all the troop dismayed, she gleaming fell!
Still radiant in the sunbeam's bright embrace:
And crushed—a little hearts-ease in her fall.

Part II

And lo! bewildered, tranced as in a dream,
The wondering band too late remained; for Day
Surprised them with his fatal, fiery glance,
And from that hour, they vanished from the earth!
Yet ere they passed away—to our lost Lulin
Outspake her fairy majesty—and calm,
And cold her sentence fell, as falls the snow
On some young flower:—"Soars the sprite so high?
Her pride shall have due deference.—Henceforth,
A diamond shall our Lulin's prison be,—
A palace rarely carved and lighted up;
Nor shall the culprit liberty regain,
Till, set in ring of gold, she goes to grace
The finger of a maid, whose dainty love,

Like hers, disdains all fellowship with earth,
And soars to meet some spirit of the skies.
When that maid shall forego her airy dream
To wed with clay,—the spirite, her penance o'er,
Her sin forgiven, shall fly her diamond cell."

"The tale is told.—To Lilith's care,
I give my lovely, diamond sprite,
My prisoner fay, with golden hair,
And tiny wings of purple light,
And cheek of rose, and eyes of blue,
And fluttering scarf of emerald hue;

But I've a faint misgiving, sweet,
That still the wilful lovers meet!
Methinks 'twere sweet to watch all day,
The sunbeam flirting with the fay!
And oft I've seen some radiant thing
(That waved so fast its flashing wing,
Its shape escaped my dazzled eyes.—
Perhaps her lover in disguise!)
Into the diamond palace dart!
And sudden, waking with a start,
My sprite, that lay so still and cold,
Flings back her locks of gleaming gold,
Waves her bright wings, in glad surprise,
With radiant blush and beaming eyes;
And with her light scarf, strives to chain
Her brilliant guest,—Alas, in vain!
Recalled, to heaven her angel flies,
And all the diamond's rainbow dies!

So Lilith, take the culprit fay,
And let her have her fairy way.
Think—how would you like, thus to pine
Within a prison, lady mine?
Recall your soul to things below,
And let the dainty creature go;
And while you set one subject free,

Another captive take—in *me!*
Believe me, you, whose spirit now
So coldly looks from eye and brow,
If once you let Love's heavenly ray
Glide in upon your heart to play,
Would wake like her to glorious bloom,
And all your lovely cage illume;
And *not* like her, the hapless sprite,
Should *Lilith* mourn her lover's flight!"

Young Lilith took the diamond ring,
And while she watched the fairy's wing
Within it play, she listened, mute
And blushing to her lover's suit.
Ah! woe the morn sweet Lilith gave
Her troth to him—the minstrel brave!
The bridal now was scarcely said,
Ere from the gem the fairy fled.
And as she glanced like light away,
In Lilith's dark eyes paled the ray;
And ere the sprite was lost to view,
Her cheek had changed its glowing hue;
Her eyelids closed!—can it be death?
Ah, Heaven that fluttering, failing breath,—
The fay has fled—and Lilith's soul,
Too pure for *this* world, heavenward stole!

Notes

Since in the narrative I am, in part, going over familiar ground, I have not here felt it neccssary to dwell on items that are already well known. My chief concern is with laying out and discussing the particular documents on which my main argument is based, and generally I detail my reasoning. No item is overlooked, however, which forms a link in the chain of primary evidence. Sources are given mostly in short form and may be fully identified by reference to the Bibliography. For *The Broadway Journal,* frequently mentioned, I use the initials *BJ.*

1.
REGION OF SIGHS

The February 28 lecture was reported the next day by a dozen New York papers, at various lengths and in various moods. The substance of the lecture is from the newspaper accounts, from Poe's own comments in *BJ,* March 8, 1845,

and from his views expressed elsewhere. His opinion of
Fanny Osgood is from a review he wrote a few months later
(*BJ,* December 13, 1845).

William Gillespie's meeting with Fanny after the lecture
is from his letter, quoted in my text (Griswold Mss., Boston
Public Library). It is my personal conviction that Fanny's
first interest in Poe was ignited by literary ambition, even if
that interest quickly became personal. Poe had been familiar
with her work since accepting some of her poems and stories
for *Graham's Magazine* as early as 1842, though he had not
then met her.

The Poe houses in New York City are described in
Beecher, "About New York with Poe," and in Phillips, Vol.
II, passim.

Fanny Osgood

It is a pity that Fanny's biography was never written, and
the fact that it was not—considering her contemporary fame
and the qualified writers who were eager to do it, Miss
Lynch and Mrs. Oakesmith, for instance—gives reason for
pause. What prevented its appearance? Was it her friends'
fear of calling too close attention to a character thought spot-
less, but which had finally been soiled by scandal? As it is,
the sources are very scattered. I have relied mainly on the
following: a "Memoir" by Rufus Griswold in *International
Miscellany,* December 1850; two memorial volumes edited
by Mrs. Hewitt, containing prose, poetry and reminiscences:
The Memorial, 1850, and a revision, *Laurel Leaves,* 1854;
articles by Elizabeth Oakesmith in *Beadle's Monthly,* January 1867, and *Baldwin's Monthly,* September 1874, as well
as her *Autobiography,* 1824; three reviews by Poe: *BJ,* December 13, 1845, *Godey's Ladies' Book,* September 1846, and
Southern Literary Messenger, August 1849; a brief memoir
in *Book of the Lockes,* 1853; an article by Ellen Ballou in
New England Galaxy, Winter 1963.

In addition to the above, Fanny figures in a number of

books by or about the literary figures of the period, particularly *Poe's Helen* by C. Ticknor; *Two American Pioneers*
by M. Wyman; *Rufus Griswold* by J. Bayless; and *Selections
from the Correspondence of R. Griswold*, edited by R. Griswold, a nephew.

Also, I have consulted the small collection of Osgood
papers at Houghton Library, Harvard, consisting mostly of
letters *to* Fanny. Among these, very interesting is a series of
nineteen, written in the short space of six months by Hiram
Fuller, later editor of the New York *Mirror,* whom Poe was
to sue for libel in the English matter. Fuller reveals himself
as one of Fanny's most persistent admirers and this may have
played its part in the role he later took against Poe, acting
out of resentment and disgust at what he and many others
saw as Poe's seduction of Fanny. Other sources, for more
particular items regarding Fanny, are cited at pertinent
places below.

"He regarded his wife with fondness. . . ." from the short
story "Florence Errington," by Fanny Osgood, *Graham's*
February 1845. The subtitle she gave the story is instructive:
"An O'er True Tale." There is also in the story a passage
which may refer to Sam Osgood's philandering: "He became
careless and frequented his club, and grew fond of gay
parties. . . . He met one night a brilliant and impassioned
creature . . . and he was soon a willing victim to the beautiful and gifted coquette." Sam's particular coquette, according to Mabbott (*Poems,* p. 556) was Elizabeth Newcomb,
sister of a friend of Ralph Waldo Emerson. The fact that
there was a breach in the first place between Fanny and
Sam was also recorded by Mabbott, which is supported by
a number of Fanny's poems, as well as the fact that the two
were apart during most of 1844-45.

Just when in 1844 the separation occurred is unclear, but
perhaps it was during the summer. One of three surviving
letters of Sam to Fanny shows that in April 1844 Sam was
away, doing a portrait in Baltimore. It also seems to show

that, on the surface at least, there had as yet been no break
between them. However, the phrase near the end of the
letter, beginning "Oh my dear Fanny . . . ," may indicate
there had already been some strain. The letter follows (the
reader is warned that Sam was not enamoured of punctua-
tion).

                          Baltimore Sunday April 17 1844
I am once more in the city of Monuments my dear blessed
Fanny and have received a warm welcome from a great many
kind friends among them Mrs. [illegible] and family, many of
the Hofmans and a great many others my fingers ache from the
pressure they have received. Mrs. Sarah [illegible] is quite
angry because I did not bring you with me she really seemed
to feel very disappointed so have several others everybody
enquires particularly after you and the children. Mrs. [illeg-
ible] is very well and sends love. Miss Hancock of Boston
with her father and brother [two words illegible] staying at
[illegible] where I am for the present but must go elsewhere
during the convention because I wont pay $2 a day. I have
your story from Alexanders express Messenger. I did not see
Patterson of the Saturday Post but I left a note requesting
him to send the $25 to me. I have the paper with [three words
illegible] which I will send to you, with this. I am sorry that
you did not get some little trifles for presents to those that
you intended should have them here. If you can afford it
buy one of those ornaments in imitation of the Egyptians at
Tiffany or Youngs, for Mrs [illegible]. You can get one of
this shape [small sketch here] for $1, with a green [illegible]
running round it it will please her more than any other thing
just because no one else has one here. Or there is one of the
same price in the form of the cornucopia they are dark
brown you must buy a little box to put it in and pack it
with cotton—you can get a box at the grocers for a shilling
send by Harndens express if you get it.
   My darling I have felt very homesick since I left but I
feel better now and when I get to work I shall be happier I
hope. I went to the office this evg to get [illegible] letter to
comfort me but it is not to be had I have had three invita-

tions to dinner to-day but I did not feel in spirits to accept so I dined at home.

Alexanders said that the [illegible] were not any of them worthy of the prize according to the Committee's notion so it was not awarded. I will send it some convenient opportunity but you must alter the title if you publish it. What did dear little Ellen say when she found that I was gone God bless you all Oh my dear Fanny how kind you have been to me the last six weeks I love you dearly for it. Write me immediately darling kiss the children for me and believe me ever affectionately your husband   S. S. O.

(Osgood Papers, Houghton Library; for Sam's other two letters see pp. 143-45.)

"The finest intelligence that . . ." —Griswold, *International,* December, 1850.

"Yes, always by the dull . . ." —Oakesmith, *Beadle's,* January, 1867.

"a weird tender child whom . . ." —Oakesmith, *Beadle's,* January, 1867.

As an example of many similar comments on Fanny's personality, here is Rufus Griswold: "In her manners there was an almost infantile gaeity and vivacity, with the utmost simplicity and gentleness . . . astonishingly impressible faculties . . . exquisitely sensible to applause." Griswold also records how Fanny's determination at times to give up living in hotels and boarding houses, and set up housekeeping on her own, became "fit occasions for jesting . . . she was not indeed fitted for such cares." (*International Miscellany,* December 1850).

The word "infantile" was also used by Tom English in his oft-quested description of a soiree at Anne Lynch's house: "At my feet little Mrs. Osgood, doing the infantile act, is seated on a footstool, her face upturned to Poe, as it had been previously to Miss Fuller and myself." (*Independent,* October 15, 1896).

"a heart so radically artless . . ." —*Godey's*, September, 1846.

Fanny's reaction to the burning of the Providence neighbor's barn is from a letter of Hiram Fuller, November 21, 1842 (Osgood Papers, Houghton Library). Her reaction to the friend's admonishment at the party is from Oakesmith, *Beadle's*, January 1867.

"I know my soul is strong . . ." —from Fanny's poem "Aspirations," as reprinted in *BJ*, December 13, 1845.

The account of the first meeting between Fanny and Poe is woven from two sources: Fanny's own account to Griswold (*Memoir*), and her fictional rendering of the moment in her short story "Ida Grey," published in *Graham's*, August 1845. The passage "I do not think I ever . . ." is from "Ida Grey." I take it that, at this juncture, the relevance of "Ida Grey" needs no demonstrating. See an incidental reference to it by Poe in 1848, where he tells Mrs. Whitman that the story had appeared in *Graham's*, August 1845 (Ostrom, p. 411).

"He spoke in a low voice . . ." —Oakesmith, *Baldwin's Monthly*, September 1874. She also recalls an instance of Fanny's specific reaction to Poe's conversation: "I have seen the childlike face of Fanny Osgood, suffused with tears under this wizard spell."

"The fair, fond girl who . . ." —*BJ*, April 5, 1845. To this coy hint Poe responded a week later in *BJ* with a sonnet entitled "To F - - - -." and signed "E." Fanny must have been greatly pleased, especially since she could not have known that this particular sonnet ("Beloved, amid the earnest woes") had done amatory duty twice before, with young ladies in Baltimore and Richmond. (See Mabbott, *Poems*, pp. 235-37).

I am inclined to think that one of the chief places of meeting for Fanny and Poe in the first weeks of their friendship was the Park Theater, during the run of Mrs. Mowatt's comedy, *Fashion*. There was great interest in the play and Poe paid it a good deal of attention in *BJ*, but his admission that "we have been to see it every night since its first production," (*BJ*, April 5, 1845, p. 219) means that he was there *ten* nights running, beginning on March 25. The crowded Park, of course, would have made a quite innocent rendezvous.

"For hours I have . . ." —Griswold, *Memoir.*

"Great self control and no . . ." —This fragmentary note in Fanny's hand, scribbled on an envelope in pencil now much faded, is preserved with her papers at Houghton Library. It may have been jotted down as part of some story she was drafting, but that it refers to Poe, I feel, is certain— in fact it could very well be a cancelled passage from "Ida Grey." The postmark on the envelope is May 4, 1845, about two months after their first meeting.

The Forgery Charge

Curiously, no Poe biographer has yet placed the forgery charge, and its attendant events, in its proper 1845 setting. All mention it only in passing, in connection with "The Literati" of 1846 or the lawsuit of 1847. My treatment of it is derived from analysis of the primary documents printed in Moss, *Crisis,* as follows: English's attack on Poe in response to the "Literati" piece (New York *Mirror,* June 23, 1846), pp. 36–37; Poe's reply to English (*Spirit of the Times,* July 10, 1846), pp. 57–59; English's deposition in the lawsuit, pp. 167–68, as well as some of the other papers in the suit, pp. 171–75, 177.

At the trial, Edward Thomas took the stand to testify on Poe's behalf, corroborating his letter of retraction. Then in a letter to Fanny (dated March 15, 1847) he managed to make light of the whole matter:

> You know the result of Poe's suit vs. Fuller. It went as I thought it would for I always believed the article a libel in reality. I had strong apprehension that your name would come out under English's affidavit in a way I would not like for I believe Poe had told him things (when they were

friends) that English would swear to, but they left the names blank in reading his testimony so that a "Mrs. _____" and "a merchant in Broad St." were all the jury knew, except on the latter point which I made clear by swearing on the stand that I was "the merchant in Broad St." I got fifty cents as a witness for which sum I swore that Poe frequently "got drunk" and that was all I could afford to swear to for fifty cents. (Moss, *Crisis,* 181–82).

It is not probable that Thomas or his friends would have wholly invented so specific a crime as forgery. What they heard, undoubtedly, was a rumor that reached back over a decade to Poe's relations with his foster-father in Richmond, a rumor spread by Allan's second wife and her sons, no friends of Poe. It was said by them that during the days of his poverty in Baltimore, Poe had forged Allan's name, probably to some sort of financial document (Harrison, pp. 112–13). In discussing this, Woodberry (I, pp. 102–3) admits that Poe's enemies were the source, but adds that in Richmond "a rumor of forgery had long been orally known." Such a rumor, spread by the second Mrs. Allan, would not be surprising—in a letter written as late as 1881 she says that everything she has heard of Poe "was a tissue of ingratitude, fraud and deceit" (Quinn, p. 206). While the exact truth of all this will probably never be known, its importance here is the surfacing of the old talk in New York in 1845. How it reached Thomas and Park Benjamin, and exactly what they heard would be interesting to know, but nothing of this remains.

The fact that English strongly urged Poe not to drop his suit against Thomas, and Poe's reply to this, is in Moss, *Crisis,* pp. 58–59, 167–68. It is transparent, from the documents that the two did get into a heated argument over it.

The Chivers–Poe Incident

My main source for this episode is Chivers's own accounts printed in *Century Magazine,* October 1909, and Winwar,

Palace 279–81. It is Chivers who records the incident of Poe, on the sidewalk, being hailed from the doorway of a saloon. He does not identify the man in the doorway but since the dates of the forgery affair and the Chivers incident agree so very closely, I conclude that the hailer was indeed English. (Discussion about hiring the lawyer was recorded by English, *Independent,* October 29, 1896.) Chivers leaves no doubt that Poe was staggering drunk, so I have assumed that he had just left the saloon, which Chivers locates in Nassau Street. Dates have been determined by analysis of Chivers's account in *Century,* and Poe's own statements (Moss, *Crisis,* pp. 57–59). These show that Chivers met Poe in Nassau Street on June 29 or 30, and that Poe left for Providence, probably on July 2. The forgery affair began during the week of June 16, when Fanny told Poe of the Thomas charge, and it was just about two weeks later when he decided to seek the services of a lawyer.

Poe's July Visit to Providence

Poe said that after hiring the lawyer, "I left town to procure evidence." (Moss, *Crisis,* p. 58), and that when he returned he found waiting for him at home the letter of apology and clarification from Edward Thomas. That letter is dated "New York, July 5, 1845."

Poe's later poem *"To Helen"* contains the reference to a walk on a "July midnight" (past the home of Helen Whitman in Providence). A passage in a letter of Poe's to Mrs. Whitman (Ostrom, II, 384) shows that he was not alone: "You may remember that once, when I passed through Providence with Mrs. Osgood, I positively refused to accompany her to your house." Griswold (*Memoir*), who had his information from Fanny, confirms all this. And there is further confirmation in an 1865 letter of Helen Whitman in which, purely by chance and in passing, she records the not irrelevant fact that Fanny and Poe were staying at the same hotel: ". . . Mrs. Osgood, who was at the hotel in Providence, where Mr.

Poe stopped on that 'July midnight'." (The whole letter is
quoted in Miller, *Biography*, p. 218.)

I place Poe's return from Providence on July 6 because
he was not at home to receive the Thomas letter on the
fifth, and he certainly could not have gotten copy ready for
the *BJ* issue of the twelfth if he had returned much later
than the sixth. For this issue he was in sole charge, Charles
Briggs having retired from the magazine while Poe was
absent.

That Fanny left New York for Providence in mid-June
1845, a date that tallies with the start of the forgery affair,
is established by analysis of letters with their postmarks,
written to Fanny at the time (Osgood Papers, Houghton
Library). She was back in New York by early August.

Stoddard and Poe

The incident involving R. H. Stoddard at the *BJ* office
is from Stoddard's own accounts in *National Magazine*,
March 1853; *Lippincott's*, March 1889; *The Independent*,
June 24, 1880; and his 1903 autobiography. Poe's two notices
to Stoddard in the "Correspondent's Column" of *BJ* appeared July 26, 1845, p. 47, and August 2, 1845, p. 63.

The reference to Fanny Osgood in this connection is not
reported by Stoddard, and is the one item in my narrative
lacking a documentary basis. But to someone immersed
in *all* the documents and the surrounding events, it becomes
an irresistable probability. Stoddard nowhere gives sufficient
reason for Poe's getting angry enough to threaten him physically, and I am convinced that Stoddard is leaving something
out, something he *said*, that prompted Poe's instant resentment. The visit took place just when Fanny's story, *"Ida
Gray,"* was the talk of the town—it had appeared less than
two weeks before—and Stoddard was one of Fanny's admirers. Stoddard later covered up other facts in his relations
with Poe (for instance, that he had once written Poe asking

for an autograph) and I offer the reference to Fanny as the necessary link he omitted here.

About a year later Stoddard took a petty revenge on Poe when he rejected "Ulalume" for the *Union Magazine,* pretending he found it gibberish (Mabbott, *Poems,* 412). I suspect, however, he may have been aware of the poem's connection with the child, Fanny Fay, and declined it on that account. See below, pp. 146-48.

The Boston Lyceum Hoax

The leading facts about Poe's appearance in Boston are sufficiently well known. What has never been dealt with adequately are the two seemingly divergent claims:

1. Poe's definite statement that the use of "Al Aaraaf" was intended as an outright hoax *(BJ,* November 1, 1845).

2. Fanny's statement that Poe asked for her help in composing a new poem for the event (Griswold, *Memoir).*

My version of the incident attempts to reconcile these claims, both of which I believe to be true.

The two weeks afforded Poe to prepare for the Lyceum is an estimate, derived as follows: according to Poe, the invitation arrived "a month or six weeks" after he gave the manuscript for his new volume of poetry to the publisher *(BJ,* December 13, 1845, p. 358). This date is shown by a covering letter to have been September 10, 1845 (Ostrom I, p. 297). Six weeks from September 10 cannot be correct since the Lyceum date itself was October 16, and a month also seems too much, since that would have given less than a week for preparation. I have thus compromised on the first days of October.

That "Lulin" was written by Fanny at Poe's request, for delivery at the Lyceum, is stated unequivocally by Griswold, who had it from Fanny herself *(Memoir.* Griswold slants the incident against Poe, making him plead for Fanny's help). When Poe asked Fanny to do a poem for him, he would hardly have left entirely to her the choice of subject, and the topic chosen makes it certain that Poe suggested it. Fays and fairyland, in fact, were just then on his mind, since in *BJ*, October 4, 1845, he had reprinted his own sketch, "The Island of the Fay." The link with Drake's *The Culprit Fay* is too obvious to require proof—and in fact in "Lulin" Fanny employs Drake's title exactly:

> So, Lilith, take the culprit fay,
> And let her have her fairy way.

Of course, Poe never recorded his disappointment over "Lulin." But anyone who reads the poem today will agree that it could not have been so different from what I suggest. "Lulin" was published in Sartain's *Union Magazine* in two parts, May and July 1848 (not May-June, as in Mabbott, *Poems*, p. 559). It consists of 130 lines, but Griswold (*Memoir*) says this printed version was only "a fragment of what she wrote." I can discover no reason why Sartain might have held the second part of "Lulin" out of the June issue, not printing it until July. Was there something in that second part that Fanny, or Sam, at the last moment found a little too revealing, and wished to have deleted or changed?

Poe's letting the cat out of the bag at the supper after the lecture was recorded by Poe himself, *BJ*, November 1, 1845. By October 18 the *Boston Transcript* had published the facts on "Al Aaraaf," having done some quick research after hearing from someone present at the supper of Poe's drunken admission.

I will not insist overmuch on Poe's intention with regard to Bailley's *Festus*. However, the English epic had recently been published by a Boston firm and had taken the east by storm, as earlier it had taken England. Poe had read it, at least read in it, in August 1845. He reviewed it briefly and favorably in *BJ*, September 6, 1845, promising to return to a fuller consideration later, which he never did.

There is one small question which might seem to loom large as an objection to the theory that Poe conceived the "Al Aaraaf" hoax while he was in Providence with Fanny, and only after her poem, "Lulin," had proved a disappointment. Where would he have obtained a text of the old poem at such short notice? It had been printed in a volume only twice (1829, 1831) and he would hardly have had either of those old books in his possession at the time. But that objection, by sheer happenstance, is easily disposed of. When Poe left New York for Providence he took with him the proofs of his new volume of poetry (*The Raven and Other Poems,* published by Wiley and Putnam in November 1845) which contained the full text of "Al Aaraaf." He later said he was reading these proofs "on the evening before" he appeared on the Lyceum stage (*BJ,* December 13, 1845, p. 358).

Poe's Stopover in Providence, October 17–20

My estimate that Poe left New York for Providence and Boston on October 13 and did not reach home until the twenty-first is founded on his own statement that the trip to Boston occupied a week (Ostrom vol. 2 p. 298). There is also his admission that the preparation of the *BJ* issue for October 25 was done in an unusual hurry (*BJ,* November 1, 1845) which would not have been the case had he returned to New York directly after the Lyceum appearance. That he spent the days after the sixteenth with Fanny in Providence is another surmise—not so wild a one, I think, since he would have passed through Providence on his way home, and there is no indication that he spent them anywhere else.

Fanny's presence in Providence at this time is shown by the letter she wrote on October 21, 1845, headed "Providence, City Hotel, Tuesday." (Osgood Papers, Houghton Library), and there is additional evidence in letters addressed to her then. The letter of October 21 was written to George Graham in Philadelphia, asking that he return a

sketch "about a literary soiree in N. Y. which I don't want
you to publish. . . . There is something in it—which it has
just struck me—might be misinterpreted." In exchange for
the sketch she enclosed the manuscript of "Caprice," which
Graham published in his February 1846 issue.

That Fanny was talking of herself in "Caprice" was recognized by Graham, who in his reply a week later says,
"Caprice," I will keep for *Graham's*. Why should I not
since it is so pretty a portrait of the writer?" (Osgood Papers,
Houghton Library) .

The Child Fanny Fay

Nowhere in all the published reminiscences and memoirs
of Fanny Osgood's contemporaries can I find the slightest
mention of the child Fanny Fay, though Fanny Osgood herself is frequently named, along with her other two daughters.* Yet Fanny Fay's existence was certainly known, for
her Providence friend, Mrs. Brown, in a letter of July 20,
1846, three weeks after Fanny Fay's birth, remarks: "Your
little one shall be Fanny; what a charming name you have
given her." Again, four months later (December 1, 1846) ,
Mrs. Brown writes, "Tell me, too, something respecting
Ellen and May, and that dear little Fanny Fay, too; has she
grown? Or is she going to be a little fairy?" (both letters in
Osgood Papers, Houghton Library) .

The only occurrence of the child's name in print in the
nineteenth century, so far as I can find, was a single line in
1853 in *The Book of the Lockes*, a geneological record
(Fanny Osgood was a Locke) . After the listings for the Os-

---

*There is, however, one veiled reference in Griswold's biographical
sketch of Fanny, published in the *International Miscellany*, December 1850. He writes that Fanny was buried in Mt. Auburn Cemetery,
Boston, "beside her mother and her daughter." The sketch was printed
before the deaths of either of the other two daughters, Ellen and May,
both of whom died in 1851.

good daughters, Ellen and May, giving dates of birth and death, this occurs:

Fanny Fay, b.   in New York, d.

Just why the information could be obtained for Ellen and May but not for Fanny Fay, is a matter of legitimate curiosity. In 1900 a history of the Osgood family (a widespread clan) listed Fanny Fay as "born June 1846, d. October 28, 1857)." The year of death was later corrected by Mabbott to 1847 (*Notes and Queries,* January 10, 1931) which is corroborated by the records of Mt. Auburn Cemetery, Boston (information courtesy of Ellen Ballou). Then the child was forgotten until 1969 when Mabbott (*Poems,* p. 557) in discussing Fanny and Poe observed: "The paternity of Mrs. Osgood's third child, Fanny Fay . . . has been questioned, although perhaps not in print," No one, including this author, has been able to turn up a birth record for the child. For more on Fanny Fay, see below, pp. 139, 146-47.

Fanny Osgood's Poems in BJ *November-December 1845*

After her return to New York from Providence in early November 1845, Fanny published a number of poems in *BJ*. They do not, in my view, carry the importance usually assigned them (see for instance, Moss, *Battles*, pp. 208–17, and Winwar, pp. 273–85). One poem printed November 22, ("Oh, they never can know that heart of thine,") is vague enough to refer to anyone, and in fact one of its phrases, "beauty and grace," would not seem to indicate Poe. The lines are just the sort of trivia that Fanny reeled off by the yard, addressed to her dozens of friends. Another, printed November 29, ("I cannot tell the world how thrills my heart,") does refer to Poe, but it is a perfectly honest tribute to his volume of poems, just then published. A third, printed

December 13, ("I launched a bark on Fate's deep tide,") is another objectless indulgence in lovelorn sentiment, an excise in metaphor, though just possibly it may be intended as a mournful comment on her own marital troubles. A fourth, printed on December 20 and entitled "To the Lady Geraldine," I agree probably refers to Mrs. Ellet, but not in her supposed capacity as a rival for Poe's attentions. More likely, it is Fanny's admonishment to Mrs. Ellet for taking a leading part in all the gossip about her and Poe.

The other anonymous verses attributed to Poe by Mabbott (*Poems*, pp. 382–86), as belonging to this literary bundling, I must reject. Their relevance is hard to discern, and even at his worst Poe could never have written such flat stuff.

Fanny's Visit to Amity Street

The date of Fanny's visit to Amity Street (her sketch in Griswold, *Memoir*) has always been accepted as spring 1846 because of the reference to Poe as just then finishing the "Literati" papers. Yet Poe was not at 85 Amity when he completed the "Literati," but at Fordham, and he probably did not even begin writing the series until after leaving Amity Street, in mid-February. The "Literati" sketch of Fanny appeared in *Godey's* in September 1846, in the fifth instalment of the series, so it could have been written as late as early June. What Fanny was shown on this visit must have been the long review of her work that Poe published in two parts—in *BJ*, December 13, 1845 and in *Godey's*, March 1846. Writing four years later about her visit, when she herself was in the latter stages of her last illness, it is not surprising thàt she confused this earlier review with the later "Literati" excitement. Almost certainly, the visit took place in late November or early December 1845.

The long extract from Poe's first review of Fanny's works (the volume published by Clark and Austin, New York, 1845) is from *BJ*, December 13, 1845, pp. 353–55.

Poe and Virgina

The circumstances surrounding Poe's marriage are worthy of lengthier analysis than they have so far been accorded. I am concerned here, however, mainly with supporting the tradition that Poe and Eliza White had reached at least a tentative understanding, and that it was Mrs. Clemm's interference that brought about the marriage to Virginia.

Against this theory, biographers always cite two items:

1. The well-known letter written by Poe in Richmond to Mrs. Clemm in Baltimore, on August 29, 1835, about a month after he had taken up work on the *Messenger*. In it he declares his passionate love for Virginia and his hope to make her his wife (Ostrom, vol. 1, pp. 69–71).

2. The marriage license taken out by Poe in Baltimore on September 22, 1835, for himself and Virginia, but not used until later.*

In light of these two undoubted facts, Poe's later statement that "I did violence to my own heart, and married for another's happiness, where I knew that no possibility of my own existed," (Ostrom, vol. 2, p. 393) is usually rejected as an embarrassing falsehood, unworthy of a gentleman. But always overlooked in judging these facts are the circumstances that called forth the 1835 letter and the license, and the amount of time that passed between them and the actual marriage. Alone in a drab Richmond boarding house, Poe received the news from Mrs. Clemm about Neilson Poe's offer to take Virginia into his family. He saw himself losing the only home he had, of which, after much roaming, he had been a part for nearly five years. In that situation his letter of August 29 can be seen as his anxious and lightly considered response to this new threat to his happiness. The marriage license was his guarantee to Mrs. Clemm that a union would eventually take place—after all, Poe was asking

---

*The old assertion that a marriage did take place in September 1835 I cannot accept on the evidence. The view of Quinn, pp. 227-28, appears to be the correct one.

his aunt and her daughter to sacrifice what would have been a very comfortable life with well-off relatives.

But between the time he returned to Richmond with Mrs. Clemm and Virginia, in October 1835, and his marriage in May 1836, he experienced seven months of a wholly new existence. Both socially and professionally those seven months saw the blooming of Poe's personality and confidence, and it was during this time that the intimacy with Eliza White ripened. Very soon, I would say, he began to regret his impulsive commitment to his aunt and cousin. I for one am willing to accept his later claim that he married Virginia to maintain his honor, out of what he himself called a quixotic sense of chivalry (Ostrom, vol. 2, p. 393) , and under pressure from Mrs. Clemm, which he does not mention.

The conjectured understanding with Eliza White, and Mrs. Clemm's interference on Virginia's behalf, are mentioned in most biographies, though sometimes with a demur. See especially Weiss, *Home Life of Poe,* pp. 74-79, and Mabbott, *Poems,* pp. 545-46.

The two-year abstinence from marital relations was twice mentioned by Poe in conversation, both times in the latter half of 1848. The first admission was to the brother of Annie Richmond, along with the claim that in marrying Virginia he had "yielded to the solicitation of friends." (*New England Quarterly,* September 1943) The second was made to Mrs. Oakesmith (one wonders under what circumstances) and was recorded by her in a letter to J. H. Ingram. (Mabbott, *Poems* p. 523)

Poe's story, "Eleonora," which certainly incorporates a memory of the period when the two-year abstinence was terminated, was first published in fall 1841; its date of composition is not known. The two years were up in May 1838, when the Poes were living in New York. By coincidence, a description of Virginia by a fellow boarder at this very time still survives. It shows the child-wife to have matured considerably, and to be acting like any blooming bride. The boarder describes her as "of matchless beauty and loveliness; her eye could match that of any *houri,* and her face defy the genius of a Canova to imitate; a temper and disposition of surpassing sweetness; besides, she seemed as much devoted to him as a young mother is to her first-born." (Allen, p. 339)

Virginia's Letter to Fanny

The fact that at some point Virginia went so far as to write a letter to Fanny Osgood, urging the woman to accept her husband's friendship, was twice asserted by Fanny herself. Virginia implored her, she says, to "be kind to Edgar, to grant him my society and, to write to him, because she said, I was the only woman he knew who influenced him for his good. . . . He wrote to me, imploring me to love him, many a letter which I did not reply to until his *wife* added her entreaties to his, and said that I might save him from infamy, and her from death, by showing an affectionate interest in him." (Griswold, *Correspondence,* p. 186.) A second reference occures in the sketch she supplied for Griswold's *Memoir*: in this she claims that she maintained a correspondence with Poe "in accordance with the earnest entreaties of his wife, who imagined that my influence over him had a restraining and beneficial effect."

Just when in 1845 Virginia's letter to Fanny, now lost, was sent cannot be determined. It may be that it was prompted by a poem of Fanny's that appeared in the *Broadway Journal,* August 30, in which she denounces certain slanderous gossip and expresses concern with the injured party in a triangle. The publication of these lines, at this time, when "Ida Grey" was causing so much talk, can hardly have been a coincidence and Virginia must have read them with great interest.

> A whisper woke the air,
>   A soft light tone and low,
> Yet barbed with shame and woe;
>   Now might it only perish there,
> Nor farther go!

Ah me! a quick and eager ear
   Caught up the little meaning sound:
Another voice has breathed it clear,
   And so it wanders round
From ear to lip, from lip to ear,
   Until it reached a gentle heart,
And *that*—it *broke*.

It was the only heart it found,
   The only heart 'twas meant to find,
When first its accents woke;
   It reached that tender heart at last,
And *that*—it broke.

Low as it seemed to other ears,
   It came—a thunder-crash to hers,
That fragile girl so fair and gay,
   That guileless girl so pure and true . . .

To these sentiments, the letter that Fanny describes as coming from Virginia would have made an appropriate response. It would have been hard for Virginia, in any case, to have read these lines without seeing herself as "that fragile girl."

2.
REGION OF WEIR

The soiree at Anne Lynch's house, 116 Waverly Place, less than a five-minute walk from 85 Amity, took place on January 10, 1846. The date, those present, and the incident with Margaret Fuller, have been derived by analysis of Didier, p. 12; Whitman, p. 37; Gill, p. 321; Ingram, p. 293; Ostrom vol. 2, p. 310. A dissertation by Jane Ball Davidson, "Margaret Fuller and Edgar Allan Poe: A Relationship Between Literati," American University, 1967, has also been of assistance.

The letter of Mrs. Brown to Fanny, dated February 21, 1846, is in the Osgood Papers, Houghton Library.

Poe's article on Fanny in *Godey's*, March 1846, could have been completed no later than the middle of January, and most probably was written much earlier, say about the same time as his previous review in *BJ*, December 13, 1845. It continues his comments on her Clark and Austin volume, and offers a lengthy discussion of her first published book of poems, which came out in London in 1842. In *Godey's*, quoting from among the poems in the English volume, he couldn't resist the urge to give a passage in which occur the following lines (from "Elfrida," written about 1841):

> My haughty, glorious, brave, impassioned Edgar!
> Well I remember when these wondering eyes
> Beheld him first—I was a maiden then,
> A dreaming child—but from that thrilling hour,
> I've been a queen in visions!

He also quotes Edgar's reply:

> Earth hath no language, love, befitting thee!
> For its own children it hath pliant speech,
> And mortals know to call a blossom fair,
> A wavelet graceful and a jewel rich—
> But thou!—oh, teach me, sweet, the angel tongue
> They talked in heaven, ere thou didst leave its bowers
> To bloom below.

Elfrida expresses a fear that her husband may overhear them talking in this manner, and Poe quotes Edgar's answer:

> Name not the felon knave to me, Elfrida;
> My soul is flamed whene'er I think of him.
> Thou lov'st him not? Oh, say thou dost not love him!

The Ellet Affair

No single incident in Poe's life, of comparable importance, has remained so obscure for so long as the puzzling affair of the Osgood letters, which gave rise to the actions of the vindictive Mrs. Ellet. In Poe's own day there were floating rumors about these incidents, and even veiled references

in the newspapers (see Moss, *Crisis,* pp. 86-222 *passim*).
Every biographer since then has referred to them, yet without
dispelling the confusion—all the more remarkable because
it is generally agreed that just here lies the key to much of
the vilification that has dogged Poe's reputation ever since.
The hidden factor, I am convinced, was Fanny's pregnancy
and the accompanying belief among the New York Literati
that Poe was the father. It was felt by many that sweet trust-
ing Fanny had been cruelly seduced, taken brutal advantage
of, by the arrogant Mr. Poe, while his own poor wife lay
on a sickbed at home. Only when Fanny's pregnancy is
applied to the known and familiar facts does the whole matter yield to the light. At this time, late January 1846, the
pregnancy was about three months advanced, and it was
now that the affair of the letters occurred, bringing in its
train the Ellet-Lummis excitement.

In the narrative, I have attempted to show, in detail, how
each subordinate development must have flowed from and
contributed to the others. In these Notes, where the source is
given as "author's conclusion," I intend this to mean that
the item does not depend on one specific document, but was
derived by analysis of all the evidence, answering to the
triple pressures of fact, necessity and probability.

Virginia's finding of Fanny's letter to Poe: Partially author's conclusion, but that she had possession of it is clear
from Mrs. Ellet's letter of July 8, 1846, see text, p. 69. Because of its nature I think the letter came to Virginia's hand
by accident.

The contents of Fanny's letter: Partially author's conclusion, but controlled by the fact of the pregnancy itself,
and by Mrs. Ellet's letter to Fanny (see above) in which
she refers to "fearful paragraphs . . . which haunted me
night and day like a terrifying spectre." It was these fearful
paragraphs that were the basis for Mrs. Ellet's later gossiping, spreading what Griswold called "foulest calumnies"
and "actionable things of Mrs. Osgood and E. A. Poe."

(Phillips, p. 1146). From the whole tenor and tendency of the many sources I have studied, it is abundantly clear that Fanny's letter to Poe contained something a good deal more serious than amorous endearments. I conclude that it was an announcement of her pregnancy, at least that the pregnancy was mentioned in some revealing way.

Mrs. Clemm's visit with English and Mrs. Ellet: Recorded by English himself, *Independent,* October 29, 1896. Her meeting with Mrs. Ellet is partially author's conclusion, controlled by Phillips, pp. 1141-50, and Winwar, pp. 229-301. That Mrs. Ellet, armed with righteousness and sisterly concern, went straight to Fanny to report how her letters to Poe were being misused is recorded by Mrs. Whitman: "She called on Mrs. Osgood, remonstrated with her on her imprudence, prevailed on her to break off the correspondence, and obtained her consent that a committee of ladies should demand in her behalf the return of the letters." (Ticknor, p. 101). This is supported by what Poe wrote later to Mrs. Whitman: "The only one thing for which I found it impossible to forgive Mrs. O. was her reception of Mrs. E." (Ostrom, vol. 2, p. 408). The controlling factor lurking silently in the background, of course, was Fanny's pregnancy. Without some such factor of overriding importance, why would Fanny have needed "a committee of ladies" to obtain the letters? If it were only a matter of unguarded correspondence why could she not have handled the matter herself? Why let others in on the delicate business? She must have known that the delegation of women descending suddenly on his home would be taken by Poe as a serious affront. Something else, something left unspoken, was the mechanism that prompted Fanny to agree with Mrs. Ellet. That something, undoubtedly, was Fanny's distressing knowledge that her secret had been discovered. For no other reason, I believe, would she have subjected Poe to such an indignity.

Visit of Lynch and Fuller to the Poe home: This is given in most Poe biographies, often with incorrect elements. I have used, particularly, Ostrom, vol. 2, pp. 407-8; Ticknor, pp. 100-1: Moss, *Battles,* pp. 217-19; and Reece, *American Literature,* March 1970. Whether there really were letters to Poe from Mrs. Ellet, of a definitely compromising nature, is something that can probably never be settled. She vigorously denied it, of course, and the only surviving notes of hers to Poe deal with the editorial matters of the *Broadway Journal,* to which she occasionally contributed. One note, written December 16, 1845, contains a postcript in German: "I have a letter for you—will you be so kind to call upon me this evening after 8 o'clock and take the letter or send for it." (Griswold Mss., Boston Public Library, and see Ostrom, vol. 2, p. 409). Probably Mrs. Ellet did write mildly flirtatious letters to Poe, of a sort she might easily shrug off later, but in the hope of attracting the critic, not the man. It is easy to see how Poe, angered, might describe such letters as compromising.

Poe's voluntary return of the Ellet letters: Ostrom, vol. 2, pp. 407-8; Moss, *Battles,* pp. 218-19; Reece, *American Literature,* March 1970. I have assumed that Mrs. Ellet was living at her brother's house on Broome Street (New York City *Directory,* 1846).

Lummis's notes to Poe: Author's conclusion, necessary in the nature of the case.

The Poe-English encounter: Reported by English in the *Independent,* October 29, 1896. My description of the fight carefully reflects English's own account. That English had a height and weight advantage over Poe is clear from a description of him even in old age as "tall and well built" (Quinn, p. 349), which means he was perhaps a 180-pound six-footer. Poe stood a slim five-eight, weighing about 150 pounds. After the fight, of course, both men claimed victory. English insisted that he had given Poe such "severe treatment," that the effect of the blows had confined him to bed. (Moss, *Crisis,* pp. 35, 37). Poe retorted that it was he who had bestowed on English a "fisticuffing," and that he had to be "dragged from his prostrate and rascally carcase." (Moss, *Crisis*, p. 52).

Virginia's reaction to the fight with English and the Lummis threat: Author's conclusion, but offered with firm certainty as the hidden reason for Poe's sudden and surprising apology to Mrs. Ellet, and for his leaving Amity Street. I am also firm in my belief that this was the beginning of Virginia's final illness; see particularly Poe's own later remark that Virginia "on her death-bed declared that Mrs. E. had been her murderer." (Ostrom, vol. 2, p. 408). That Virginia's reaction to Poe's condition on reaching home that day centered on the lacerated cheek, is an obvious point that has been overlooked. It must have been an ugly cut. The ring was a heavy seal, an intaglio, and the impact of the blow knocked the stone from the setting. (English, *Independent*, October 29, 1896).

The part played by Dr. Francis: Moss, *Crisis*, pp. 37, 92, 196; also mentioned in Griswold, *Memoir*, and most Poe biographies. It is my own conclusion that the doctor was called into the matter in the first place to attend Virginia, not Poe, and that it was he who advised Poe to send Mrs. Ellet the letter of apology, suggesting the grounds of temporary insanity. Mrs. Ellet made quick use of the letter—the papers as early as April reported rumors to the effect that Poe had "become deranged," or was suffering from "brain fever," and was about to be confined. (Moss, *Crisis*, p. 92).

Dr. Francis in his reminiscences, *Old New York*, makes no mention of Poe, though he does refer to many of Poe's contemporaries. In the *Memoir* of Dr. Francis by Henry Tuckerman that prefaces the volume, there is a brief scene that well may describe the very night, in early February 1846, on which Poe first went to fetch Dr. Francis for Virginia. Tuckerman was among the guests at Francis' house one evening when the servant unexpectedly announced Mr. Poe. "Dramatically entering a strange circle," Poe was introduced by Dr. Francis as "The Raven!" and shown round the table.

He held a private conference with Francis and then left. After he went, some wit in the company solemnly and rather cruelly quoted Goldsmith: "Remote, unfriended, solitary, slow . . . wandering Po." Objectively this was a clever hit, and it soon gained currency among the literati. Hiram Fuller used the line in the *Mirror*, July 20, 1846 (see above, p. 65, and Moss, *Crisis*, p. 70) , and Evert Duyckinck quoted it in his article on Poe in *Cyclopedia of American Literature*, 1851. Tuckerman, in his Francis memoir, makes another slight, and erroneous, reference to Poe. In the course of praising Dr. Francis' charitable nature, he says: "Some of his experiences with the unfortunate votaries of pencraft would afford subjects for Dickens and Disraeli; he remembered Weems pedalling his *Life of Washington,* carried food to Selleck Osborne in jail, relieved Freneau's indigence and Poe's mania. . . ."

Poe's letter of apology to Lummis: The original of this important letter long ago disappeared and no copy was made, or none has been found. Its general substance, however, is easily inferred from the various sources cited in the foregoing, as well as Mrs. Ellet's letter to Fanny Osgood of July 1846 (See pp. 69-71).

Date of the move from 85 Amity Street to Turtle Bay: All the evidence (see particularly Reece) shows that the Ellet affair took place in late January-early February 1846. That the move from 85 Amity Street did not happen until after mid-February is shown by Virginia's valentine to Poe, the envelope for which is addressed to 85 Amity (Phillips p. 1096, where it is given in facsimile) . But that the move took place very soon after mid-February is indicated by Poe's statement of April 16, 1846: "I have been living in the country for the last two months" (Ostrom, vol. 2, p. 313) .

Poe's 1846 Valentine to Fanny

On February 14, 1846, Anne Lynch gave her annual Valentine's Day party, for which each guest was expected to contribute verse valentines to be read aloud. A week later some of these verses were printed in the *Mirror*, among them one of Poe's to Fanny. Neither had attended the party and just how Poe's offering found its way into the *Mirror* is not known. The poem must have been written and sent to Anne Lynch some time before. It was a complicated piece that would have required time to write (concealing Fanny's name, as it does) and certainly it was composed before the visit of Lynch and Fuller to 85 Amity Street in late January or early February. Probably it was not read at the party at all, and its use in the *Mirror* may have been due to the paper's editor, Hiram Fuller, who wanted to honor Fanny, no matter the source.

A sidelight on the end of the affair between Fanny and Poe is incidentally set forth in two letters to Fanny written by Mary Neal, daughter of critic John Neal. The letters show that soon after the Ellet business, when the pregnant Fanny was again under the care of her husband, she offered to give away a lock of Poe's hair. On February 23, 1846, Mary Neal wrote Fanny asking for a lock of *her* hair. In her reply Fanny suggested that her young admirer might also like to have a similar memento of Poe. On April 25 Mary answered enthusiastically, "I guess I *do* want a lock of Mr. Poe's hair! I guess I *am* an admirer of his *Raven!*" (Both letters in Phillips, pp. 1100-1). Poe must have given Fanny the lock sometime before, since she could hardly have meant that she would approach him then, after the unpleasantness with the Ellets. Also, by this time she no longer met the Poes.

"The Literati"

My treatment of the "Literati" series in *Godey's* (May-September 1846) intends to show that the Ellet affair had its first public repercussions in this connection, and that Poe's deplorable exchange with English and the subsequent lawsuit also had their roots in the Ellet business. The whole "Literati" imbroglio, and the lawsuit, may be followed minutely through the original documents reprinted in Moss,

Crisis; see also Moss, *Battles,* pp. 221-48; Quinn, 501-6; Woodberry, vol. 2, pp. 186-95.

That Poe felt considerable chagrin at the *Mirror*'s personal description of him (printed in its issue of May 26, 1846, quoted from Moss, *Crisis,* p. 14), which almost no reader would have taken seriously, can be seen in his pathetic effort to counter it. On June 15 he wrote his St. Louis friend, editor Joseph Field, asking that he "say a few words" condemning the description, "to do away with the false impression of my personal appearance it *may* convey . . . you have seen me and can describe me as I am. Will you do this act of justice, and influence one or two of your editorial friends to do the same? *I know you will.*" (Ostrom, vol. 2, p. 319).

Mrs. Ellet did not find a place in the "Literati," though Poe had planned to include her, and might have done so if the series had extended further. His short, subtle treatment of her was left in manuscript and was published after his death in *Works.* To appreciate the piece, it should be recalled that Mrs. Ellet was a well-educated, highly regarded serious writer of fiction, non-fiction and poetry, whose work appeared frequently in many magazines and books, and that she was also young and attractive:

> Mrs. Ellett, or Ellet, has long been before the public as an author. Having contributed largely to the newspapers and other periodicals from her youth, she first made her debut on a more comprehensive scale, as the writer of *Teresa Contarini,* a five-act tragedy, which had considerable merit, but which was withdrawn after its first night of representation at the Park. This occurred at some period previous to the year 1834; the precise date I am unable to remember. The ill success of the play had little success in repressing the ardor of the poetess, who has since furnished many papers to the magazines. Her articles are, for the most part, in the *rifacimento* way, and, although no doubt composed in good faith, have the disadvantage of *looking* as if hashed up for

just so much money as they will bring. The charge of whole-sale plagiarism which has been adduced against Mrs. Ellet, I confess that I have not felt sufficient interest in her works to investigate—and am therefore bound to believe it unfounded. In person, short and much inclined to *embonpoint*.

Poe did not invent the charge of plagiarism against Mrs. Ellet—though the "wholesale" was his own deftly malicious touch. In *BJ*, February 15, 1845, p. 109, many months prior to their falling-out, he *defends* Mrs. Ellet against such a charge from an unnamed source. He provides little detail, but apparently the charge concerned an article of hers which carried her name as author, but which was in reality a translation.

The article "A Sad Sight," (*New York Mirror*, July 20, 1846) is quoted from Moss, *Crisis*, p. 69-70.

Birth of Fanny Fay

The two poems "Fanny's First Smile" and "Ashes of Roses," are quoted from Fanny's 1850 volume, published by Carey and Hart in Philadelphia. Whether these two pieces were printed elsewhere prior to their appearance in this 1850 volume, which was prepared by Fanny herself just before her death, I have not been able to discover. (No other poem in the volume appears to have reference to the child.) The volume also contains a number of illustrations, among which are engravings of the two Osgood daughters, Ellen and May, from originals painted by their father (the portraits are not identified but accompany generalized poems on children). There is no picture of Fanny Fay.

The Poes were probably still at Turtle Bay when Fanny Fay was born on June 28, 1846. Some weeks before the birth, on June 12, Poe stayed from home overnight, and apologized for his absence in a note to Virginia (Ostrom, vol. 2, p. 318), saying that Mrs. Clemm would explain. He refers to an "interview" he has been promised, which may bring "substantial good," but this does not appear to be connected with the reason why he must remain away overnight. He closes: "I shall be with you tomorrow P.M. and be assured until I see you, I will keep in loving *remembrance* your *last words* and your fervent prayer!" The original letter, now lost, was written on a page torn from Poe's pocket notebook (Ostrom, vol. 2, p. 519). Though I have long studied this letter, I must confess that I can make nothing of it, if there *is* anything to be made of it. I can only suggest that if it is not connected in some way with the birth of Fanny Fay, then imminent, it may have to do with arrangements for renting the cottage at Fordham. But why should that keep him away overnight?

Mrs. Ellet and Fanny

Mrs. Ellet's letter to Fanny of July 8, 1846, is in the Griswold Mss., Boston Public Library.

Before we may allow the woman's chattering to fade away, there is a final dim note that should be sounded. Despite all her abject contrition and her promises to cease her gossiping forever, and despite Sam Osgood's threats to prosecute, the determined woman eventually returned to the attack. In 1849, with Sam absent in California, Fanny had to turn to Griswold for help in silencing her. Griswold accosted her in person, saying he would publish her July 1846 letter to Fanny if she did not desist. He reminded her "of the terror into which she had been thrown by Mr. Osgood's threats to prosecute her for the same tales when first uttered and of her humble retraction then made." (Bayless, p. 153; Phillips, p. 1146). This seems to have shut her up at last. But why did she resume her campaign? What facts discovered as late as 1849 strengthened in her mind the truth of the gossip about Fanny Fay's paternity? I have no answer.

A woman of rather implacable resentments, who was involved in more than one violent fuss, Mrs. Ellet lived until 1877. If her obituary in *Potters Magazine*, for May that year, may be believed, however, she was a changed person later.

The magazine, to which she had frequently contributed, said that she gave the fee for her last article to a destitute family: "She ever felt for and sympathized with frail and suffering humanity, and her open heart and hand made many a home happier." Since the woman is so unreservedly damned in Poe biography, it is pleasant to find that age may have softened her. About her brother, William Lummis, nothing further is known, except that he was sometimes called Colonel—he was a native of South Carolina, as was his sister—and that he was at this time a New York merchant with an office on Pearl Street.

Fanny Osgood in "The Literati"

In his "Literati" piece on Fanny, Poe again allowed himself an unguarded remark, one which seems to show that his personal feeling for her, despite the Ellet business, was undimmed: "Not to write poetry—not to think it, dream it, act it, and be it, is entirely out of her power." For some reason not readily apparent, he also rang in an equivocal reference to Sam Osgood. Referring to the couple's sojourn in England, he writes: "Mr. Osgood's merits as an artist had already introduced his wife into distinguished society . . . but her beautiful volume had at once an evidently favorable effect upon his fortunes. His pictures were all placed in a more advantageous light by her poetical and conversational grace." At the close of the sketch Poe writes, "Her husband is still occupied with his profession. They have two children, the Ellen and May of the poem." From this it seems the sketch must have been written in early summer, before the birth of Fanny Fay.

The "Hammerhead" satire on Poe by T. D. English ran in the New York *Mirror* between September 5 and November 7, 1846. My quotations are from Moss, *Crisis* pp. 102-3, 106-7, 119-21. Moss reprints the entire five selections, but much of the material is extraneous to the present subject.

". . . had been her murderer . . ."—Ostrom, vol. 2, p. 408.

Poe says that Virginia made the accusation "on her death-bed." He also says that Virginia was "continually tortured (although not deceived) " by anonymous letters from Mrs. Ellet, none of which have survived.

The *Morning Express* and *Bostonian* extracts relating to Poe's illness are quoted from Moss, *Crisis,* pp. 125-26.

Virginia's last words to her mother are from Mrs. Clemm's letter in Burr, *Nineteenth Century.*

Charles Briggs' *Mirror* satire on Poe is quoted from Moss, *Crisis,* pp. 199-201. The "Wicks" episode ends with a veiled allusion to Poe's "Literati" series in *Godey's,* and says that in it Poe held "poor Lizzy up to ridicule." A sketch of Mrs. Ellet was indeed written by Poe but it was not used. (See above, p. 138) . Does Briggs' statement indicate that Poe in fact meant to use it but was overruled, perhaps by Godey?

Poe's Visit to Fanny in Albany

In 1885 the Rev. Harrington, then living in New Bedford, Massachusetts, wrote a letter to *The Critic,* printed in the magazine on October 3. In it, Harrington objects to a recent laudatory article on Poe in *Encyclopedia Britannica,* which he considered a "whitewash." He complained that it erroneously presented Poe as pure, industrious and truthful, and falsely minimized his drinking. On the contrary, Harrington insisted, everyone who knew Poe was aware of his "sensual excesses," and among the examples he gives is the Albany visit. Notably absent from his short account, of course, are such things as *why* Poe should have thought that he had a chance of winning Fanny away from Sam, and *how* he knew that Fanny, without Sam, was then at her sister's place in Albany (for this I assume a letter from Fanny to Poe) . Again, it would appear that the existence of the child, Fanny Fay, underlies the whole episode, and the incident, it must be admitted, tends to establish Poe's own belief that he was the father of the ill-fated child.

The date of the Albany visit is derived from Harrington's

statement that it took place about a year after discovery of
the Poes' destitution in fall 1846. It is my own conclusion
that it occurred just before the death of Fanny Fay, mainly
because I think Poe would not have made such a visit *after*
the child's death.

Reconciliation of Fanny and Sam

Two letters of Sam to Fanny, written in the summer of
1847, are among the Osgood papers, Houghton Library.
They appear to show that the reconciliation of the two was
complete, though Sam still had to spend time away from
home painting portraits. The second letter, written some
three months before the death of Fanny Fay, reveals that the
child had been ill and had recovered somewhat but still
needed careful attention.

> Brunswick, July 6th, 1847
>
> I am anxiously looking for a letter from you my dear preci-
> ous Fanny and I hope to hear that you have pleasant rooms
> in the country for I cannot enjoy the comfort here until I
> know that you are comfortable. I thought of you all day
> yesterday as suffering in town and I was miserable when I
> [layed down?] to think of your suffering in that hot room.
> If you cannot get rooms at [illegible] do take some others
> until you can find a place out of town. Write immediately
> and tell me if you have money from Post or [illegible] that
> I may send you some if you have not. Mrs. Philbrooks bill
> need not trouble you [illegible] pay that when I come to see
> you again. I hope the children are well, kiss them for me. I
> painted all day yesterday and have got on very well so far.
> If you can without inconvenience write a piece of poetry to
> Mrs. [illegible] I wish you would for she is so kind [two
> words illegible] and trys to make me happy here. She is in
> a decline I fear. Do not mention it to anyone. Did you hear
> of that dreadful accident to Mrs. Howland's son-in-law Mr.
> Brown on Saturday last. He was lying in a hammock and his
> little brother and cousin were firing a little toy cannon
> loaded with shot. When it went off he sprang from his ham-

mock saying I am shot and died immediately. They have been married about 3 years and she is left a widow at 18. She is a lovely sweet little thing and he was an interesting young man possessing everything one could wish to make life desirable. If you find a place where there is a school near try and engage for the children for [illegible] it worries me to think that they are not getting a better education and [illegible] having more exercise. Do go out as much as you can I wish you could go ride on horseback take lessons I mean. Goodbye God bless you dear darling Fanny love to all.

                                                            S. S. Osgood

I did not suffer from the heat walking down to the cars and the ride did my head good. I was quite well yesterday and am now.

                                        New Brunswick Aug 5, 1847

My darling your letter came yesterday with one for Dr. D. Your note to him was very happily expressed and seemed to please him very much. I am delighted to hear that our dear little Fanny is better you must still be *very* careful of her. Mrs. D. has had a letter from Piermont but the house there is entirely filled up. She proposes that you all come here to her house but as Mrs. Grigsby would say "it could not be so." The Dr. [illegible] could not write his sermons with dear Fanny crying all night. If Welford has a letter for me send it immediately if it [illegible] before Saturday night. I expect one from Mrs. [illegible]. Give my love to all, dear Mrs. [illegible] in particular. Tell Miss Lynch that I should be delighted to make a drawing for her and am very much pained to think that I cannot. Tell her my eyes trouble me so much that I have not been able to read anything this 6 months and that they are particularly troublesome just now so that I can paint only an hour or so a day. Give my best love to [illegible] kiss my dear children for me and be sure and let me know as soon as you hear of any rooms. Some friend has enquired at Long Branch but there was not a bed to be found within 5 miles of the bathing place. It is too bad my darling that I cannot find a place for you any where. I should feel so much happier if I could. God bless you my darling Goodbye. Your article in Post Mag is [two words illegible].

S. S. O.

It was probably about the time of Poe's disturbing visit to Albany that Fanny wrote a short poem to her husband entitled "To S. S. Osgood," and subtitled "Suggested by an unfinished Picture." (*Literary World*, October 23, 1847, and *Works*, 1849). The lines praise Sam for disdaining to court riches and transient fame, from which it appears that Sam had not yet given up his hope of achieving something permanent in art.

Sam's return from his year in California, in late 1849, called forth another poem by Fanny, "The Return," in which, while she celebrates her renewed happiness and her reborn love for Sam, she is still bitterly reminded of the travail that had blighted her previous three years:

> No summer came while he was gone
>> But sooner than I thought,
> The blissful balm and bloom of spring
>> His sunny presence brought.
>
> Worn, weary, wasted with long grief,
>> The faith that never died
> Through all the suffering, glows again,
>> Now he is by my side.
>
> My brave, beloved wanderer!
>> He came to me like light,
> And with a sudden morn of joy
>> Flushed all the fearful night.
>
> Ah! Pain, Misfortune, Care
>> No more your flying steps I fear,
> His love has drawn a magic ring,
>> Ye cannot enter here!

Mean Envy, while your serpent-speech
  Winds hissing from those lips,
The pearls and flowers affection speaks
  Your keenest words eclipse.

Wild Hate, the child of love disdained,
  Yet mourned with pitying tears,
You cannot harm or fright me now,
  Go, rave to other ears.

False Slander, turn and sting yourself!
  Ours is a charmed sphere;
His love has drawn the magic ring,
  Ye dare not enter here.

Sweet friends; beloved and loving ones,
  The gifted, pure and true!
To heart and hearth a welcome warm,
  We still have room for *you*!

When, scared by Evil Eyes,
  Too frail to cope with coarser foes,
Your cherished one shrank mutely back
  In Truth's unreached repose.

Ye did not shrink, but shamed them down
  To Coward Falsehood's Fear;
Come, enter Love's enchanted ring,
  You're always welcome here!

These lines were published in the N.Y. *Tribune*, almost certainly in Spring 1850; I quote them from an undated clipping in the Osgood Papers, Houghton Library. (The *Tribune*, to save space, printed them as twenty long-line couplets, but they are obviously meant for quatrains.)

Fanny Fay and "Ulalume"

The suggestion that "Ulalume" concerns the death of Fanny Fay, and not Virginia or some other woman, real or imagined, first forced itself into notice because of a coincidence in dates. As is now known, the poem was written sometime in the fall of 1847 (Mabbott, *Poems,* pp. 409-12) . That the month of composition was October is implied by the poem itself, of course, but that it was certainly at least begun in that month is clear from an article that appeared in *Home Journal,* July 21, 1860 (reprinted in Laverty, *American Literature,* 1948) . This places the *reading* of the finished poem "a few weeks after" some unspecified date in September 1847. Since the death of Fanny Fay occurred on October 28, 1847, and "Ulalume" was published in the *American Review,* December 1847, there would seem enough time to fit the writing of it into the interval October 29-November 10. (The sidelights on the poem offered by the *Journal* article, and by Mabbott, *Poems,* p. 411, do not in my view vitiate the fundamental inspiration derived from the child's death.)

While it has been assumed that the occupant of the burial vault in "Ulalume" is a woman once the beloved of the speaker, this is not necessarily so. The only identification occurs in the words "thy lost Ulalume," a phrase that remains unqualified throughout the poem. The words could apply to a female of any age, and of any close relationship to the speaker, including that of daughter. That the poem, under its symbolism, does in fact record the keen stabbing of Poe's guilty conscience is suggested by a reference of Mrs. Whitman, who has preserved Poe's own admission to her that the poem was in some sense autobiographical. (Quinn and Hart, *Documents,* p. 49) .

The poem's speaker, after a veiled sexual allusion to a time when his volcanic heart overflowed with sulphurous currents—they "groan" in their slow descent—is threatened by a sudden vision of Astarte, goddess of Love. His personified soul is terrified, sobs hysterically and wishes wildly to flee the apparition. No reason is given in the poem for this sudden, strange fright, but one is needed, for the soul does not usually recoil at the advent of love—though conscience might. The speaker takes no heed of the alarm but continues to contemplate the vision not yet fully aware of its sexual nature. At length he is assailed by painful recollections—the tomb—of the awful results of his transgression, the birth and tragic death of an illegitimate child.

Naturally, in the poem these things are skillfully overlaid. And in this connection it is revealing that the tenth and final stanza, often omitted in reprintings and which Poe himself finally dropped, in its execution and linkage to the story is woefully inept. After the throbbing precision of the first ninety-four lines, the sudden falling off in those last ten lines is jarring. Does that last stanza represent a belated attempt to further bury the poem's real meaning?

Stoddard's glimpsing of Poe in Ann Street and his leaving him in the rain are reported by Stoddard himself (*Lippincott's*, March 1889). He adds that he does not know what made him hold back, though he is sure it was not done through unkindness.

EPILOGUE

That Fanny and Poe never met again after January 1846 is, from all evidence, certain (or as certain as such things can be). The statement of Sarah Whitman (Ticknor, p. 131) that Poe saw Fanny in Providence in the winter of 1849 is unsupported, and furthermore is self-serving, since it is linked to Mrs. Whitman's effort to claim "Annabel Lee" as written to herself. The assertion is contradicted by Fanny ("We met only during the first year of our acquaintance," *Memoir*), and by Griswold emphatically: "Mrs. Osgood, I am confident, had not seen him, nor written him a syllable, in more than two years." (Ticknor, p. 149). Griswold makes that assertion in a letter of December 17, 1849, written in New York, where he had begun to frequent the Osgood home. At that time Fanny had entered the final phase of her illness.

Mabbott's statement (*Poems*, p. 561) that Fanny visited the Poes in Fordham in the fall of 1846 is based on a remark in the Rev. Harrington's article that he met Fanny in New York one day when she and another woman were preparing, apparently, to go to Fordham. Harrington could easily have been mistaken about the arrangements (Fanny could have been seeing the other woman off) and no bit of evidence actually places Fanny in the Bronx cottage. I do not say that she might not have gone personally to the aid of the Poes, only that a visit is both unproved and unlikely.

That Mrs. Clemm personally destroyed Fanny's letters to Poe was stated by her in an 1860 letter to Neilson Poe: "After Eddie's death, I burned every letter except those relating to literature. I destroyed hundreds that were written by literary ladies. I know so well that Eddie wished me to do so . . . I was offered by the *base, base* man, Griswold, $500 for a certain literary lady's correspondence with Eddie. This was the reason I destroyed them, for fear I might by poverty be induced to do anything so *dishonorable*." (Quoted in Miller, *Biography*, p. 50) . That the "certain" lady was Fanny Osgood may be taken as more than probable, if not absolute.

The description of Fanny's last days is by Griswold, (*International Miscellany*, December, 1850) . Interesting, and a little puzzling, is the fact that it was Griswold and not Sam who informed Fanny of her approaching end, and that he did so by writing a letter and handing it to her.

Griswold's friendship with the Osgoods, which seems to have begun sometime in 1848, and especially his intense feeling for Fanny, have been strangely overlooked. Certainly this must have played a large and now utterly forgotten part in his personal hatred of Poe. As with Stoddard, Hiram Fuller and others, it is at last clear that Griswold never forgave Poe for what appeared to be his heartless seduction of the childlike Fanny. That is the one missing factor which alone explains his calculated rage.

One reason that so little has been known with certainty about Poe's relations with Fanny is the fact that her husband and two surviving daughters disappeared so soon from the existing record. Less than two years after Fanny's death both girls had followed their mother to the grave: May on June 26, 1851, and Ellen on September 2 of the same year. Brief obituaries in the New York *Tribune* give no cause of death for either, though it is stated that Ellen died at "the Spingler Institute." Sam Osgood remarried in 1855, lived for a time in New York, then went with his wife to California, where he died in 1885.

If Fanny found some of the passages in Poe's 1849 *Messenger* notice familiar, she would have been right. It was entirely a patchwork, which he put together by mining his three earlier reviews of her work, with the passages transferred word for word. A footnote explains: "Some passages of the above article have appeared in some of our magazines, in *Marginalia,* etc.," which was understating the case considerably. Just why Poe felt called on to publish such a rehashed review, just at this time, it would be interesting to know. Perhaps it would not be too difficult to guess—only a few months before he had broken with Helen Whitman, had not yet resumed his acquaintance with Elmira Shelton, and was alone in the world.

Bibliography

Allen, H. *Israfel: The Life and Times of EAP*, Farrar and Rinehart, 1934.

Ballou, E. "The Artist and the Admiral," *New England Galaxy*, Winter 1963.

Bayless, J. *Rufus Wilmot Griswold*, Nashville, 1943.

Beecher, J. "About New York with Poe," *The Curio*, Jan. 1880.

Benton, J. *In the Poe Circle*, New York, 1899.

Bond, F. "The Problem of Poe," *Open Court*, April 1923.

Briggs, C. "Personality of Poe," *Independent*, Dec. 13, 1877.

Briggs, C. "Poe," *Holden's Dollar Magazine*, Dec. 1849.

Burr, C. "The Character of Poe," *Nineteenth Century*, Feb. 1852.

Carlson, E. (ed.) *The Recognition of EAP*, University of Michigan Press, 1966.

Casale, O. "The Battle of Boston: A Revaluation of Poe's Lyceum Appearance," *American Literature*, Nov. 1973.

Chivers, T. "Poe," *Waverly Magazine*, Sept-Oct. 1853.

Chivers, T. *Chivers' Life of Poe*, E. P. Dutton, 1952.

Coburn, F. "Poe as Seen by Annie's Brother," *New England Quarterly*, Sept. 1943.

Derby, J. *Fifty Years Among Authors*, New York, 1884.

Didier, E. *The Life and Poems of EAP*, Widdleton, 1877.

Didier, E. *The Poe Cult and Other Papers*, Broadway Pub. Co., 1909.

Ehrlich, H. "The Broadway Journal—Briggs' Dilemma and Poe's Strategy," *Bulletin of the New York Public Library*, LXXIII, 1969.

English, T. "Reminiscences of Poe," *Independent*, Oct. 15, 22, 29, Nov. 5, 1896.

Falk, D. "Poe and the Power of Animal Magnetism," PMLA, LXXXIV, 1969.

Francis, Dr. J. *Old New York*, Widdleton, 1865.

Gill, W. *Life of EAP*, Widdleton, 1878.

Graham, G. "The Late EAP," *Graham's* March 1850.

Grant, V. *Great Abnormals: The Pathological Genius of Kafka, van Gogh, Strindberg and Poe*, Hawthorn, 1968.

Griswold, R. "Edgar Allan Poe," *International Miscellany*, May 1850. (Reprinted as *Memoir* in Poe's *Works*, 1850).

Griswold, R. "Frances Sargent Osgood," *International Miscellany*, Dec. 1850.

Harrington, H. "Poe Not to be Apotheosized," *The Critic*, Oct. 3, 1885.

Harrison, J. *Life and Letters of EAP*, T. Y. Crowell, 1903.

Hewitt, M. ed. *The Memorial* (a tribute to FSO), New York, 1850 (revised as *Laurel Leaves*, New York, 1854).

Higginson, T. "Poe," *Literary World*, March 15, 1879, (reprinted in Carlson, *Recognition*, 67-73).

Ingram, J. *EAP, His Life, Letters and Opinions*, London, 1880.

January, J. "The Child Wife of Poe," *Century*, Oct. 1909.

Laverty, C. "Poe in 1847," *American Literature*, May, 1949.

Lind, S. "Poe and Mesmerism," PLMA, LXII, 1947.

Mabbott, T. *Poems of EAP*, (with Notes and a biographical

section entitled, *Annals*) in *Collected Works of EAP,* Harvard University Press, 1969.

Mabbott, T. "The Children of Frances S. Osgood," *Notes and Queries,* Jan. 10, 1931.

Matthews, C. "Story of a Poem," (*The Raven*), *Bachellor of Arts,* Sept. 1896.

Miller, J. C. *Building Poe Biography,* Louisiana State University Press, 1977.

Miller, P. *The Raven and the Whale: the War of Words and Wits in the Era of Poe and Melville,* Harcourt Brace, 1956.

Moss, S. "Poe and His Nemesis, Lewis G. Clark," *American Literature,* XXVII, 1956.

Moss, S. "Poe's Infamous Reputation, A Crux in the Biography," *American Book Collector,* Nov. 1958.

Moss, S. *Poe's Literary Battles,* Duke University Press, 1963.

Moss, S. "Poe, Hiram Fuller and the Duyckinck Circle," *American Book Collector,* XVII, 1967.

Moss, S. *Poe's Major Crisis: His Libel Suit and New York's Literary World,* Duke University Press, 1970.

Newcomer, A. "The Poe-Chivers Tradition Re-Examined," *Sewanee Review,* XIII, 1904.

Oakesmith, E. "Autobiographic Notes: EAP," *Beadles's Monthly,* Feb. 1867.

Oakesmith, E. "Edgar Allan Poe," *Baldwin's Monthly,* March 1871.

Oakesmith, E. *Selections from the Autobiography of,* Lewiston Journal Co., 1925.

Osgood, F. S. "Florence Errington," (short story) *Graham's,* Feb. 1845.

Osgood, F. S. "Ida Grey," (short story) *Graham's* August 1845.

Osgood, F. S. *Poems,* Carey and Hart, 1850.

Osgood, F. S. Untitled sketch of Poe, in *Memoir* of Poe by R. Griswold, (see above).

Ostrom, J. *The Letters of EAP,* Harvard University Press,

1948, (reprinted Gordian Press, with *Supplement*, 1966).

Paul, H. "Recollections of Poe," *Munsey's Magazine*, Sept. 1892.

Phillips, M. *EAP, the Man*, Winston Co., 1926.

Pritchard, J. *Literary Wise Men of Gotham: Criticism in New York, 1815-1860*, Lousiana State University Press, 1963.

Quinn, A. *EAP, A Critical Biography*, Appleton-Century, 1941.

Quinn, A. and Hart, R. *EAP: Letters and Documents in the Enoch Pratt Free Library*, Scholars' Facsimile Reprints, 1941.

Reece, J. "The Ellet Letters: A Re-examination of a Poe Date," *American Literature*, March, 1970.

Sartain, J. "Reminiscences of EAP," *Lippincott's* March 1889.

Sartain, J. *Reminiscences of a Very Old Man*, Appleton, 1899.

Schrieber, C. "A Close-up of Poe," *Saturday Review of Literature*, Oct. 9, 1926.

Schulte, A. *Facts About Poe: Portraits and Daguerrotypes*, University of Virginia, 1926.

Smith, Elizabeth Oakes. *See* Oakesmith.

Stern, M. "The Mental Temperament for Phrenologists," *American Literature*, XL, 1968.

Stern, M. "The House of Expanding Doors," *New York History*, XXIII, 1942.

Stoddard R. "Recollections of EAP," *National Magazine*, March 1853.

Stoddard, R. "Memoir of Poe," *Independent*, June 24, 1880.

Stoddard, R. "Edgar Allan Poe," *Lippincott's*, March 1889.

Stoddard, R. "Edgar Allen Poe," *Scribner's*, Feb. 1891.

Ticknor, C. *Poe's Helen*, Charles Scribner's Sons, 1916.

Tuckerman, H. "Memoir of Dr. J. W. Francis," in *Old New York*, by Dr. J. W. Francis, Widdleton, 1869.

Wagenknecht, E. *EAP: The Man Behind the Legend,* Oxford University Press, 1963.

Weidman, B. "The Broadway Journal—A Casualty of Abolition Politics," *Bulletin of the New York Public Library,* LXXIII, 1969.

Weiss, S. *The Home Life of Poe,* Broadway Pub. Co., 1907.

Whipple, W. "Poe, Clark and Thingum Bob," *American Literature,* XXIX, 1957.

Whitman, S. H. *Edgar Poe and His Critics,* Rudd & Carleton, 1860.

Wilbur, R. "Introduction" to *Complete Poems of EAP,* Dell, 1959.

Winwar, F. *The Haunted Palace, A Life of EAP,* Harper Bros., 1959.

Woodberry, G. *The Life of EAP,* Houghton Mifflin, 1909. (Reprinted Biblo and Tannen, 1965).

Woodberry, G. "The Poe-Chivers Papers," *Century,* Jan.-Feb. 1903.

Wyman, M. *Two American Pioneers,* Columbia Univ. Press, 1927.

Young, P. "The early Phrenologists and Poe," *American Literature,* XXII, 1951.

Index

This index contains names of poems, subtitles, and first lines of poems mentioned in this volume.